So…You Want to See Jesus

So...You Want to See Jesus

Ira Kellman
with
Jonita Mullins

 Unless otherwise identified, Scripture quotations are from the King James Version of the Bible.

Take note that the name satan and related names are not capitalized. We choose not to acknowledge him, even to the point of violating grammatical rules.

Treasure House
An Imprint of
Destiny Image
P.O. Box 310
Shippensburg, PA 17257

"For where your treasure is
there will your heart be also." Matthew 6:21

ISBN 1-56043-773-1

For Worldwide Distribution
Printed in the U.S.A.

Dedication

To my mother, Ann Kellman, who always taught me to see the best in life.

Tribute

The idea for the cover of this book was given to me by the Lord, through much thought and prayer. I would like to thank the artist, Greg Tess, for bringing this vision into focus. It is my desire that the reader see Jesus more clearly through this work.

Acknowledgments

Because I meet so many people in my travels, I have found there are some who have the honest hearts that stand out and stay with you as true co-workers in the great harvest field. This makes the long days and plane rides shorter. The rewards of peace and joy come from their receiving my message and living it.

Carol Stephen—A faithful friend, one I know truly prays. Her support in many ways makes this message available to others.

Patty and John Crommer—Friends with the same vision as mine. They desire to see people reached and changed by the Lord. They have hearts that clearly see what must be done.

My special Austrian friends:

Renate Furtner—A great translator, secretary, and meetings coordinator without whose assistance the original tapes for this message would never have come forth. She is one of God's precious ladies.

Walter and Annamarie Furtner—Mama and Papa to me and to many others. In their lives the true service of Christlike hospitality is practiced and lived.

Martin and Mariane Wassel—My true friends, music ministers, translators, and sightseeing guides. They love to serve and desire the best for people. We've had wonderful laughing times together over cappuccino.

Walter and Sonya Kammalander—A couple I've seen grow through this message to be true lights for Jesus. They are special friends the Lord gave to me. I can feel their love whenever I'm in their presence.

My special American friends:

Nick and Jan Maddix—I appreciate their encouragement, sense of humor, and desire for me to take my ministry to the world and bring the best to people.

Debra White—My information director who tracked me down in ten countries. She's a lady who always has the right thing to say...at the right time.

Debbie—My secretary who ran the office, home, and wire service and took care of my cat, King, so I could be free to run around the globe.

Jonita Mullins—My co-writer who worked so diligently while I was abroad. We flowed as one mind to assemble this book. She's a true gift from God.

Contents

Foreword

In more than 44 years of leading others to salvation and to a deeper knowledge and revelation of Jesus, the cry of my own heart continues nonetheless to echo that of the apostle Paul: "That I may know Him..." (Philippians 3:10). In the 14 anointed and highly readable chapters of *So...You Want to See Jesus*, Brother Kellman has set forth key guideposts for keeping us on the road to knowing Jesus better, and for protecting us from ever becoming jaded or self-satisfied in our knowledge of our Lord.

Dr. Morris Cerullo
President
Morris Cerullo World Evangelism

Preface

My amazing journey took me from being spiritually blinded to knowing God and moving in the calling on my life. It has taken much courage and determination to know and see Jesus in the many ways He is to us.

We all have journeys to make. The more we thirst for knowledge in these journeys, the greater our lives will be when we discover the great truths about Jesus. We must be willing to seek, see, think, and change. To live is to change.

During my journey, God revealed Jeremiah 29:12-13 to me. They led me to want to see Jesus. Study these verses. Put them in your heart and mind. Follow their direction and make them a way of life.

The search to see Jesus is a life-long journey. It cannot be accomplished in just a moment's time. That is where many miss the greater knowledge and fuller relationship with God. We must have a heart on fire, a heart that is pliable in God's hands. Then it will be a heart full of joy in getting to know and see Jesus.

As you read this book, I encourage you to keep a pen on hand and to make notes, for you will discover many new truths. Your heart will be warmed and stirred. You will be healed in mind, body, and spirit (by His Holy Spirit). Jesus Himself will become more real to you.

Chapter 1

Clearing Our Vision

Four Faces

Thousands of people have been inspired by the sculpture of Gutzon Borglum at Mount Rushmore in the Black Hills of South Dakota. He began his work in 1927, and continued on the project until his death in 1941. The mammoth sculpture includes the heads of Presidents George Washington, Thomas Jefferson, Abraham Lincoln, and Theodore Roosevelt which were cut from the sheer granite face of the mountain.

The four men whose faces were sculpted on Mount Rushmore personified to the sculptor the founding, expansion, and preservation of the United States. Borglum wanted to carve a memorial not just to these four men, but to the ideals they represented. He believed his country needed a memorial whose size and significance would stir the patriotism of every American who saw them.

The carvings are 60 feet in height from the chin to the top of the head and can be seen 18 miles away. Even before Borglum had completed the monument, tourists were traveling to the Black Hills to see this wonder. Yet many of those first visitors didn't know what they were seeing.

In 1931, when only the Washington figure was near completion, a woman visiting the Mount Rushmore monument was asked to move her car from a restricted area. She argued for a moment, but the park officials insisted she move her car. Finally, she said, "Well, we'll just leave! That doesn't look like Woodrow Wilson anyway."

Most of the visitors, however, did recognize the face of the first President, George Washington. The Jefferson face being carved behind Washington's left shoulder caused the most confusion. One early onlooker was overheard to remark, "That is a very poor portrait of Martha."

Seeing Jesus

Not seeing clearly may be amusing at times, but often it can be a problem. Everyone needs to see clearly in life. Yet that is one of the hardest tasks we undertake.

We might see clearly one day, make the right decisions and have success in what we're doing, but the next day nothing is working right. Our spirit is clogged, our mind is not thinking clearly, and we can't see which way to go.

We all need clear vision in life. A good example is a baseball batter. If a pitch comes close to him, causing him to fall down and get dirt in his eyes, he must wipe it out of his eyes before he can continue playing. His vision is impaired and he is unable to bat without good eyesight.

Jesus had something to say about impaired eyesight in His sermon on the mount (Matthew 7:1-5). He compared judging people to having a beam in our eye while we try to get a tiny speck out of our brother's eye. He admonished us to get the beam out of our own eye so we can see clearly. Then we would qualify to help our brother clear his sight.

People judge others all the time. But, that is wrong; it's like having a log in our eye. We can't see clearly. If we want to be able to see Jesus, we must be free of those things that hinder our vision. Judging others can blind us.

We need to see the truth in a very simple and clear way. Luke 6:39 says when the blind try to lead the blind, they both fall into the ditch. There are too many "blind" people in the world, both spiritually and mentally, who don't see Jesus clearly.

Matthew 6:22 (NIV) says, "If your eyes are good, your whole body will be full of light. But if your eyes are bad, your whole body will be full of darkness." When we can see clearly, we will have light in our lives. Since Jesus is the Light of the world, when we can see Jesus clearly, there will be light instead of darkness in us.

It is far more important to recognize the face of Jesus than the faces of four Presidents carved in a stone mountain. How we see Jesus is going to affect every part of our lives. It will also determine the kind of life we will live for Him.

When we see Jesus as loving and giving, we'll receive the benefits He has for us—love, peace, joy, financial blessings, comfort, wisdom, guidance. If we don't see Jesus that way, chances are we won't receive from Him. Our lives will be limited to how well we see. If we wear blinders, we see only what is in front of us—the circumstances and situations of that moment. We don't see the whole picture of what is available to us through Jesus.

God wants us to see Jesus clearly so we can impart understanding of who Jesus is to a world that needs Him desperately. The Apostle Paul said he felt called to preach "the unsearchable riches of Christ; and to make all men see" (Ephesians 3:8,9). We have a calling to preach Christ to the world, to show others who Jesus is. We want all men to see the Lord, but in order for that to happen, we must first see Him clearly ourselves.

Different Views of Jesus

From the moment of His birth, the world reacted either positively or negatively to Jesus. In the 2000 years since, many people have seen Jesus, but not all have seen Him clearly. The gospels tell the story of Jesus' life here on earth. They show us what a varied picture of Jesus the people of His day had.

When the angel announced His birth, he said, "Call His name Jesus: for He shall save His people from their sins" (Matthew 1:21). Zacharias, the father of John the Baptist, in the prophecy he gave at John's birth, referred to Jesus as "the dayspring from on high" (Luke 1:78). He was Savior to some and the dawning of a new day to others.

The wise men who followed a star from the east were searching for the king of the Jews when they found the child Jesus in Bethlehem. When Herod the Great heard about this baby, he saw Jesus as a threat to his own throne and tried to take His life (Matthew 2:1-16).

John the Baptist proclaimed Jesus to be the Baptizer in the Holy Ghost (Matthew 3:11). Later, after Herod had beheaded John the Baptist, Herod believed Jesus was the water baptizer risen from the dead (Matthew 14:12).

The people in His home town of Nazareth saw Jesus only as the carpenter's son or the son of Mary and the brother of James, Joses, Judah, and Simon (Matthew 13:55; Mark 6:3). Yet God declared Jesus was His beloved Son (Mark 9:7).

The Samaritan woman, who met Jesus at the well of Jacob, saw Him, at first, as a Jew who had dared speak to her in public. But, as she talked with Him and He revealed His knowledge of her past, she saw Him as a prophet (John 4:5-19). Another woman, who had suffered for twelve years with a hemorrhage of blood, saw Jesus as a healer. A third woman, who had been caught in adultery, called Jesus "Lord" when He asked her where her accusers were (John 8:11).

Was Jesus king or a spoiler of kings, a carpenter or the Son of God, a prophet or a healer, a baptizer in fire or a baptizer in water, a Savior or a Lord? Many people saw Jesus as He walked among them, but most saw Him as nothing more than a fellow human being. Few looked deep enough to see His true spirit. Some of the people saw Jesus as wise and a teacher who spoke with great authority. The crowds welcomed Him into Jerusalem and declared Him to be a prophet (Matthew 21:11).

Nicodemus, the Pharisee who came to speak to Jesus late one night, saw Him as a rabbi and teacher. Nevertheless, Nicodemus didn't understand the teaching Jesus brought. He saw Jesus as a good teacher, but he didn't see Him as the Christ bringing new revelation from God (John 3:1-9).

Of course, not everyone saw Jesus in a positive light. Many of the religious leaders of that day were critical of Jesus. The scribes and Pharisees saw Jesus as a blasphemer because He forgave sins and He called God His Father (Luke 5:21; John 10:36). They called Him "a gluttonous man, and a winebibber, a friend of publicans and sinners!" (Luke 7:34).

How do you see Jesus? Do you see Him as the Pharisees saw Him or do you see Him as His disciples saw Him? The first group focused on finding fault in Him. The second group found peace, joy, healing and salvation through Him. The first group was never satisfied by Him. The second group could not hold all that He offered to them. If people don't see Him in the right way today, they still will not find satisfaction in Him.

Of all those who knew Jesus, John the Baptist understood that Jesus had come to be the sacrifice for our sins. John proclaimed, "Behold the Lamb of God, which taketh away the sin of the world" (John 1:29). Still, at one point, John needed confirmation of his vision of Jesus.

After John was thrown into prison by Herod, he sent his disciples to Jesus asking, "Art Thou He that should come? or look we for another?" (Luke 7:19). John had to be reminded of the miraculous things that Jesus had done. The Lord told these disciples to go back and tell John what they had seen Him do (Luke 7:22).

Even as Jesus died on the cross, few people could see this as His purpose for coming. The repentant thief on the cross called Jesus "Lord" when he asked to be remembered as Jesus came into His kingdom (Luke 23:40,42). The centurion who crucified Jesus declared, "Certainly this was a righteous man" (Luke 23:47). Was Jesus just a good man or was He King of kings and Lord of lords?

After His resurrection, His disciples began to see Jesus in a different light. When He appeared in the upper room and satisfied the doubts Thomas had, the disciple proclaimed Jesus to be "my Lord and my God" (John 20:28).

Mary Magdalene called Jesus "Rabboni" at the tomb after He had risen from the dead (John 20:16). Rabboni is a term carrying great respect, reverence and love. It is a more emphatic and honored term than the simple "Rabbi" most people used to address Jesus.

So there were as many different views of Jesus as there were people looking at Him. Each individual saw Jesus in his or her own way. For some, this view inspired worship and adoration; others could only criticize and find fault. How they saw Jesus determined how they received Him and what they received from Him.

Chapter 2

Come and See

How Do You See Jesus?

I preached at a church in Europe called the "Come and See" Church. I thought that was a great name. That's what our churches should be about. We should be showing the world who Jesus is and telling them what He can do for them.

The way we see Jesus will determine the way we present Jesus to others. What is your view of Jesus? This is an important question to ask. The way you answer will probably say much about your Christian life.

Many people saw Jesus do miraculous things, but they still didn't understand Him. Even the disciples were confused when they were asked to explain who they thought Jesus was. Some said He was the prophet spoken of by Moses; some said He was John the Baptist returned from the grave; some said He was the Christ. Still, none of them walked in the light of the truth because they let circumstances rob them of that light.

The more Jesus taught He was the Christ, the more people grew angry with Him. The people in His hometown of Nazareth wanted to throw Him off a hill where the city lay (Luke 4:28-29). He told them the truth, but they rose up in anger. They couldn't receive that truth.

It's the same with many people today. We have dozens of different scriptures about people seeing Jesus in a positive way—as the Dayspring, the Son of God, the healer, the master, a good teacher, Rabboni. Still, many insist on seeing Jesus in a negative way. The problem is very few people respected Him in His own day and few people respect who He is or what He says today.

See the Whole Jesus

There is a poem about ten blind men who were led to an elephant. They were asked to touch the object before them and describe it. Each man only felt a small part of the elephant and each had a different description of what they felt. The elephant was too big for them to get a clear picture by touching only a small part of the animal.

Jesus is like that. He is so big, few of us see Him as He truly is. We have to be willing to take off the blindfolds that keep us from seeing. If we don't, we will see Him only from one limited perspective.

So how do you see Jesus? Is it a clear, accurate picture? Is it a complete picture? Surely all of us need to see Jesus more clearly. Many things keep us from seeing Him as He is. We want to learn what those "blindfolds" are and we want to learn how to take them off.

Birdseye View of Jesus

I was raised in a Jewish home, so I didn't grow up hearing about Jesus. In Hebrew school I studied about Abraham, Isaac, Jacob, Moses, Joshua, David, and Daniel. I heard nothing about the greatest Jew who ever lived—Jesus. If my rabbis knew anything about Him, they didn't share it with their students. If they thought of Jesus at all, they probably thought of Him as a teacher who lived a long time ago.

After I became a Christian, I wanted to learn everything I could about Jesus. I believe Jesus is more than a teacher; He is the greatest teacher who ever taught. I believe Jesus is the wisest preacher who ever lived, wiser than Solomon. I believe Jesus was anointed by God to heal the sick. The Bible tells us in Acts 10:38 that God anointed Jesus of Nazareth with the Holy Ghost and with power and, with this anointing and God's help, He went about doing good, and healing all that were oppressed of the devil. I believe an anointed Jesus is still with us today.

Many people don't believe He is anointed. If we don't see Him as the healer today, then we don't get healed. If we don't see Him as the miracle-worker today, then we don't receive the miracles we need.

It is surprising how many people—even people in the church—don't think of Jesus as a healer or the Messiah or the Savior. But I believe He's all that and MUCH more because the Bible says it is so.

We get our picture of Jesus from the Bible. The more we understand God's Word, the better we will understand who Jesus is and what He wants to do in our lives. To see Jesus, we must take a closer look at Him through His Word.

At the beginning of the U.S. troop build-up in Saudi Arabia in 1991, during Operation Desert Shield, the United States launched a spy satellite on the space shuttle. It was supposed to be a secret mission, but it didn't take much to figure out the spy satellite was going to be taking a closer look at Iraq and Kuwait. Our military wanted access to as much information as possible before each operation of that campaign.

That spy satellite covered every inch of territory in Iraq and Kuwait. It showed the movement of troops and the damage done to military targets. I've read that it could spot the sparks from the scud missiles in Iraq as they were launched. It is a remarkable piece of technology that helped our military focus on what they needed to see.

We need to focus clearly on Jesus so we can do what He asks of us. The best way to see Him is in the description of Him in the Bible. It provides us with the direction and focus we need for seeing clearly.

Men As Trees

In Mark 8:22-26 we read the story of a blind man who was brought to Jesus. This blind man needed a miracle. He was blind physically and, perhaps, spiritually as well. Unlike many of the other blind people who Jesus healed, this man did not come to Jesus on his own seeking his healing. It is possible that this man did not "see" how Jesus could heal him. Apparently, those who brought him had a clearer vision of Jesus than he did.

Herein lies a problem many of us have. We may be able to see with our physical eyes, but we can't see Jesus doing a miracle in our lives. We don't see Jesus clearly, as a healer and as a miracle-worker.

Jesus took the blind man by the hand and led him out of the town. He took him away from the critical crowds to a quiet place. He spit on the man's eyes, put His hands upon him and asked him if he could see anything. The man looked up and said, "I see men as trees, walking." Even after this first touch from Jesus, he wasn't seeing clearly.

Jesus was not discouraged. He put His hands on his eyes again to allow more anointing to flow into this man. When the man looked up a second time he could see everyone clearly. The anointing power of God breaks the power of sickness and sin. Isaiah 10:27 says, "The yoke *(which represents a burden)* shall be destroyed because of the anointing."

I encounter many people in the audiences of my meetings who won't come forward to be prayed for even though they are burdened with a sickness or affliction. They were prayed for once before and they think it is a lack of faith to receive another touch. Since their pastor or a well-known evangelist has already prayed for them, they won't receive anyone else's prayers. I say, "You need another touch so the anointing can flow into you."

It is not a lack of faith to receive a second touch (or third or fourth or however many it takes). If it were, then Jesus would not have given us this example. But many people don't see it that way. Those who do see it come forward and get the anointing and they receive the healing they need.

There are a great number of people today who also have a problem with blurry vision in the spiritual realm. We need the hand of God upon us to help us see. We need to focus upon the Word of God so we no longer see in a blurry or distorted way.

Why are so many experiencing distorted vision? We don't stay before God until we can see clearly. We don't read the Bible consistently to know what it is actually saying. That's why we get in trouble by the things we say. If we are seeing wrong, we are going to be saying wrong, and then we are going to be receiving wrong. That is why it is so important for us to see clearly.

This man saw men as trees and that's what he said to Jesus. It is not a lack of faith to admit that not all is clear. We should tell Jesus how it is with us. We should ask Him to help us with the things that are wrong. Jesus doesn't want to leave us where we are. He wants us moving on into better things with Him. If we have a problem with something, we can take it to Jesus. Jesus didn't leave this man standing there seeing trees walking around. He touched the man again and this time his sight was completely restored.

Does Jesus want to leave people today with distorted sight? No! It is a terrible strain and terribly frustrating not to be able to see. I'm blessed with good eyesight, but I know that poor vision can make life difficult. If that's true with physical sight, it is also true with spiritual sight. Too many people settle for a first touch from God but never press on to get an ever-clearer vision of Him.

God's Desires

Most people don't know that God has desires. There are things God wants to accomplish. Next to His desire for all people to enter into His salvation, He wants to help people see Him clearly and help them know Him more intimately. God doesn't want to be a mystery to us. He wants us to see Him the way He is.

Jesus doesn't want to leave us in the dark. He doesn't want us to see important spiritual matters in a blurry or distorted way. Jesus wants us to see the truth about Him, about ourselves, and about life. He wants us to see clearly so we can think clearly and have success and victory in life.

Jesus said He came to give us a life filled with abundance (John 10:10). According to James 1:17 the abundant life includes every good and perfect gift. Blurry vision under any circumstance isn't a good and perfect gift, and God doesn't want to leave us without clear vision.

He doesn't want us to "see men as trees walking." He doesn't want us to see half the sun or only part of the beautiful scenery around us. He wants us to see it all and enjoy it all. And He wants us to see all of Him. He wants us to see Him as the answer to any need in our lives. He wants us to see Him bigger than any problem we might face.

Optical Illusions

You've probably had the experience of driving down the highway and seeing the heat waves shimmering above the asphalt ahead of you. It looked as if a great body of water lay right in your path. But of course, it was all an optical illusion. There was no water there; it was only a trick of the sun and the heat.

Life is full of optical illusions. Illusions can be fun in a magic show. There are smoke and lights and mirrors, pretty ladies sawn in half, and disappearing elephants. Magicians are often called illusionists because with their sleight of hand and use of mirrors they can easily fool the eye.

We expect to be fooled at a magic show or in a house of mirrors. We enter into the fun of the illusion and enjoy the experience. But illusions aren't always fun. There are times when not seeing clearly can be inconvenient or even harmful. We think we see something as it is, but it's really not what we are seeing at all.

Many things in life are optical illusions. The devil is good at creating illusions that can fool God's people. The Bible says he can appear to be an angel of light (II Corinthians 11:14). His illusions are against the mind's eye for the mind is the arena in which satan works against us. Satan creates illusions and whispers lies.

He does that not only through the mind, but by using people as well. Unfortunately there are many con men whose "sleight of hand" can be deceptive. They want to deceive us for their own gain. It's an optical illusion that can fool the mind. That's why so many people get taken by different types of fraud.

Satan doesn't want us to see God as He is. That is because when we truly see God, when we see His love and grace and power, we are drawn to Him. The devil will do what he can to stop people from coming to God.

I have friends who are well known and often have articles written about them in the newspapers and the tabloids. Some of these stories are accurate and fair. Others are little more than fiction. The way my friends are portrayed is, often, opposite from their true character. Also, anyone who knows them knows these stories are not true. But many people believe what has been written, so they see my friends in a negative way.

I was watching a late night talk show on television not long ago. One of the guests on the program was a football player who had a reputation for being a troublemaker. He had missed several games because of a knee injury and rumors swirled that he was faking the injury to try to get traded to another team. But this running back insisted he was very misunderstood. “I’m not at all like the stories they write about me,” he said.

Words and images in the media can be very deceptive. They can create optical illusions in the mind. No matter what type of person you are, not everyone is going to see you in a true light all the time. In fact, the more people talk about how good you are, the more someone is going to try to find out what’s wrong with you.

Volumes have been written and said about Jesus down through the centuries—some of it true, some untrue. Controversy has raged around certain portrayals of Christ in books and movies. Thousands of works of art have been done through the years portraying Christ as the different artists saw Him. Jesus has had His admirers and He has also had His critics. His critics have worked very hard to find something wrong with Him.

All of this has made it difficult for people to see Jesus clearly. Many people talk about Jesus today, but very few people talk about Him the way He really is.

Through ignorance or deception, people have made false statements about the nature and character of God. Many have said, “God put me in a car wreck to teach me something" or "God gave me cancer to teach me something." It's not true! Nowhere in the Bible does it say God is going to use a tragedy as a method of instruction. The way God has chosen to teach us is by His Word and His Spirit.

The reason people make wrong statements is they do not see God clearly. When we experience problems we often blame God. God's way is to take the circumstances of life and create good from them. Sometimes that good might be a lesson we need to learn, but it is wrong to conclude God sent the problem to teach the lesson. He simply turns those bad circumstances to our best advantage. That's the kind of God He is.

That is how we need to see Him—not as others have chosen to portray Him, but as He has revealed Himself through His Word. Every human being needs expansion of his or her vision. Jesus wants to open our spiritual eyes and also our mind to understand Him more. He wants people to see Him the way He really is.

It is essential to see Jesus clearly if we are to give others an accurate picture. We want people to know Jesus is alive in us; we want them to see Him as a loving, giving, miracle-working Savior. Our goal is to "make all men see" (Ephesians 3:9).

How do we do this? First we have to set our eyes upon our goal. Hebrews 12:1-2 says, "Let us with patience run the race that is set before us, looking unto Jesus, the author and finisher of our faith." We must make this our prayer:

> "Father, I come before You in the name of Jesus. God, I want to see Jesus clearly in everything and in every way. Make Your Word clear to me. Speak to my heart clearly. I want to hear Your voice. Open my eyes that I might see Jesus. In Jesus name, Amen."

We must see Jesus as our Savior, our Lord, our healer, our strength, our friend, our redeemer, our righteousness, our sanctifier, as the God who supplies all our needs, as everything He is and everything we need Him to be. When we see Him clearly in each individual area, we will be able to receive from Him in those areas. If we can't see Jesus clearly in a particular area, then the need we have in that area is liable to go unmet.

Seeing Jesus clearly is an important part of our Christian life. It makes the difference between living a so-so life and living the abundant life. We want to see Jesus as He is—in all His greatness and all His glory. Only then can we see ourselves as God intends for us to be.

Chapter 3

The Desire to See

The First Step

The first step in learning to see Jesus clearly is to have the desire. Without a genuine desire to get to know the Lord, we won't make much progress. There are too many people in the church who are only going through the motions of attending church or paying tithes or doing the other things "good Christians are supposed to do." Still, if there is no sincere desire within our heart to know God, we will never see Jesus and never progress very far in our Christian walk.

A desire is a deep longing, a craving or strong hunger, a wish or a request. When we desire something, we are willing to pay a price to get it. Desire goes beyond wishful thinking or polite "wouldn't-it-be-nice" lip service. A desire says, "I'm going to do whatever is necessary to receive."

It takes this kind of determination to see Jesus clearly. We have to want it more than we want the things standing in our way. We have to be willing to work a little, change a little, give up a little. In Psalm 51:6, the Psalmist, tells us, "Behold, thou desirest truth in the inward parts: and in the hidden part thou shalt make me to know wisdom." The truth we must desire is to see Jesus the way He is. We must want it way down inside our spirit if we are going to make it a reality.

The Psalmist also wrote, "There is none upon earth that I desire beside thee" (Psalm 73:25). He had made a determination to know God. God promises to reward such determination by fulfilling "the desire of them that fear him" (Psalm 145:19). Jesus put it this way: "What things soever ye desire, when ye pray, believe that ye receive them, and ye shall have them" (Mark 11:24).

There are many examples of desire and determination during the ministry of Jesus in the New Testament. In Matthew, chapter 9, two blind men were determined to receive their sight. They followed Jesus crying out for mercy. When Jesus had reached His destination, the blind men came to Him. To discover the level of their faith and determination, He asked them if they truly believed He could heal them. When they replied, "Yes," He touched their eyes and said, "According to your faith be it unto you." The men received their sight.

On another occasion, Jesus was near Jericho when a blind beggar pleaded for mercy. Though the crowd told him to be quiet, the beggar persisted in his plea and, after Jesus had determined his faith and desire, the man was healed (see Mark 10:47-52).

Spiritual Sight

Each healing recorded in the New Testament tells us much more than the fact that the physical body was healed. The people who received physical healing had a desire to be healed and a measure of faith to receive the miracle. The men who received their sight were able to see with their eyes, but they had something more than physical sight, they also had spiritual sight. That is what this book is about—spiritual sight—and just as these men wanted their physical sight restored, we have to *want* to see before we can receive spiritual sight.

If we're crying out today to see, then we will see. But, in the church today, very few people truly want to see. Bartimaeus, the blind beggar, wanted to see and he was willing to cry out to God in order to receive his sight. We have to be willing to do the same thing today.

Often, we must be willing to go out of our way in order to see. While Moses tended his father-in-law's sheep (Exodus 3:1-22), he saw a bush burning. He had the desire to find out what was going on and so he took the time and made an effort to see this sight. If Moses had not turned aside, he wouldn't have had the "burning bush" experience. Because of Moses' desire to see, God revealed Himself to Moses. Moses was able to see far more than just a burning bush. God gave him a glimpse into the future.

We must turn aside from everything going on around us to see the truth for ourselves. It is then that God will respond. When we have turned aside to see and to seek His counsel, He will do something to help us see. When God sees we are making the effort to read the Word, to walk in love, to forgive, to have the right heart attitude, He responds to us and reveals Himself to us.

We have to persevere in order to see. Details in life will fall into place as we trust the Lord as our source, as our peace, as our healer. We have to do what God tells us to do. Moses took the first step to turn aside to see. When God saw him take that first step, then God took the other steps. He gave Moses a miracle, revealed His name to him, told him his calling, and gave him the power he needed to fulfill his calling.

Our physical sight is very valuable to us. Sometimes, to make this point in my meetings, I will ask, "How many people would like a million dollars?" Nearly every hand will go up. But, if I said, "Okay, how many people would give their eyes for a million dollars?" every hand will go down very quickly. They want the million dollars, but they want their eyesight even more. Their eyes are more valuable to them than money.

What we value we will pursue and we will take care of what we value. We take care of our sight because we value it so highly. We should value our spiritual sight (or insight) even more highly and should be willing to do whatever it takes to keep it sharp and clear. The beginning of the whole process is wanting to see in a spiritual way.

Chapter 4

Believing Is Seeing

I am sure you've heard many people say, "If only I could see a miracle, then I would believe in God." Even the people in Jesus' day said that—right after He had performed a miracle! The scribes and Pharisees kept asking Jesus for a sign to prove He was who He said He was. They thought if they could see a specially-ordered miracle, then they could believe. Yet they and thousands of other people saw Jesus do miracles and most of them still didn't believe.

After Jesus had fed more than five thousand people with just five loaves of bread, the crowds began to follow Him. But, Jesus said to them, "Ye seek me, not because ye saw the miracles, but because ye did eat of the loaves, and were filled." They replied, "What sign shewest Thou then, that we may see, and believe Thee?" The miracle of feeding them had not been enough to convince them Jesus was sent from God (see John 6:26-30).

Few people believe in God because of miracles. Jesus is still here, by His Spirit, and He still performs miracles today. He loves people today. He saves people and brings peace, love and joy today. But, even the people whom Jesus has blessed with miracles don't always see Him clearly because they don't believe.

Believing Comes First

The world says, "Unless I see, I won't believe." And the world doesn't see. Even at Christmas, the world doesn't see Jesus. As Christians, we learn we must believe first, then we will see. If we want to see Jesus, we must believe in Him. We must take a step of faith.

Jesus said to Thomas, "Blessed are they that have not seen, and yet have believed" (John 20:29). Thomas wanted physical proof. He wanted to see evidence he could touch before he could believe. According to Jesus those who believed without physical proof are the ones who are blessed.

Believing first is the problem for many people where faith is concerned. We want proof; we want evidence for our faith. We want to see before we risk believing. Many times people have told me, "I would believe in healing or miracles if I could just see one. But I just can't walk by faith, believing in something I don't see."

I ask, "Do you believe in heaven?" Almost always they will say, "Yes, of course."

Then I tell them, "But you haven't seen heaven, you haven't seen your name in the Lamb's book of life, you haven't seen the streets of gold, and you haven't seen the gates of pearl. You believe all this exists because the Word of God says it does. You believe it and someday you're going to see it because you have believed."

Why do we believe in heaven if we can't believe in miracles on earth? Heaven is more incredible than money, a job, or a car. Yet, we believe we'll spend eternity in heaven some day, but we can't believe God wants to provide good things for us here and now.

We believe in heaven because the Word says it is real and we believe the Word. Everything in life should work that way. Romans 10:9-10 says if we believe in our heart and confess with our mouth that Jesus is the risen Lord, then Jesus is our Lord. If we believe in our heart and confess with our mouth He's our healer, we get healed. If we believe in our heart and confess with our mouth other promises from the Bible, then, in time, we will receive them.

We have to know the Word of God is the final authority for our faith. If we can trust what it says about heaven, we can trust what it says about healing. If we can trust what it says about salvation, we can trust what it says about miracles. Either it is all true, or none of it is. Everyone has to grow into the knowledge of that truth and believe it. Only then will we be able to see Jesus and the things Jesus can do for us in the here and now.

Why is it easier to believe the things that are far away and in the future? It is because we don't have to make adjustments to it now. We don't have to make a commitment to do something in order for heaven to be real. It doesn't require any action on our part to believe heaven exists. Believing in heaven is easy, so we don't demand proof that it is waiting for us.

It requires both faith and courage to say, "I believe Jesus is a healer. I believe Jesus blesses those who serve Him. I believe Jesus still works miracles today." When we believe in Jesus and in miracles, then we see Jesus and miracles. God's way is different from the world's. When we believe God's Word, He'll show us its reality.

What we believe in life is what we will receive from life whether it is negative or positive. We must believe each promise Jesus made to us if we expect to receive the benefits of those promises. In spiritual matters, believing is seeing and seeing is receiving.

Everything We See

If we have to see everything we believe, then we will not believe much of what the Bible says. Our spiritual life will be very shallow—if it exists at all and, if we believe everything we see, we're going to believe some things that aren't true. Believing only what we see or everything we see can be misleading.

For example, I enjoy photography and subscribe to a photography magazine. The centerfold shot in one issue showed an aerial view of a sewage treatment plant. It looked beautiful from the air with the colors of the green water, the rich, brown dirt, the white smoke and the blue sky. But, from a more realistic perspective, down below, I'm sure it didn't look (or smell) too good.

Another example happened while I was watching a football game one evening. The score was close and the home crowd was excited. They were on their feet as one player scrambled down the field, broke out into the open, and dashed into the end zone for a touchdown. From the camera angle showing the play, I was as sure as the crowd that a touchdown had been made.

But another camera showed the player stepping out of bounds before reaching the end zone. The officials looked over the instant replay and then called the ball back to the place where the player had gone out of bounds. It had been an illusion. Everyone thought they had seen a touchdown, but it wasn't. Things aren't always the way they appear. Something can look beautiful or appear correct, but, in reality, it may not be. It's better to believe the truth from God's Word and want to see it come to pass.

Just Speak the Word

Once we learn to trust the Word of God, we can learn to use the Word as we exercise our belief, increase our faith and begin to see more clearly. In Matthew 8:5-13, we read the story of a Roman centurion who understood the power of God's Word. He came to Jesus seeking help for a servant who was gravely ill. The soldier was not Jewish and he probably didn't know anything about the Jewish Messiah. But, the centurion had heard interesting things about the miracles Jesus performed and he believed what he had heard.

Jesus said to the man, "I will come and heal him." The centurion said:

> *I am not worthy that thou shouldest come under my roof: but speak the word only, and*

my servant shall be healed. For I am a man under authority, having soldiers under me: and I say to this man, Go, and he goeth; and to another, Come, and he cometh; and to my servant, Do this, and he doeth it. When Jesus heard it, he marvelled, and said to them that followed, Verily I say unto you, I have not found so great faith, no, not in Israel" (Matthew 8:8-10).

Faith is what moves the hand of God and the Roman soldier had a tremendous faith in Jesus. He recognized that Jesus only needed to speak and the disease which tormented his servant would have to obey. He saw clearly that Jesus has all authority.

That's what people in the Body of Christ today need to see concerning Jesus. We need to recognize that just a word from Jesus can change anything in our lives. If we had this kind of faith in Jesus' authority, we would see more miracles today.

Believe in the Authority

The centurion believed in the authority of Jesus. We have a problem with that in the Body of Christ. We don't believe in the authority of Jesus and the power of the Holy Spirit. We don't believe in the power of prayer. God wants to deliver, but we don't believe enough to get delivered.

We have to believe Jesus has authority. If we don't believe He has the same authority now that He had when He was here on earth, how can we come to Him with our requests? How can we believe our prayers will be answered? It takes just as much authority to bring miracles to us as it did to heal the centurion's servant.

The President of the United States has authority as the commander-in-chief of the armed forces. After Iraq's invasion of Kuwait, President Bush called his generals and said, "Send our troops out." What happened? Thousands of soldiers, airmen, and sailors were on their way to Saudi Arabia because the President has the authority to send them.

Philippians 2:9-11 tells us Jesus has an even greater authority. "Wherefore God also hath highly exalted Him, and given Him a name which is above every name: that at the name of Jesus every knee should bow, of things in heaven, and things in earth, and things under the earth; and that every tongue should confess that Jesus Christ is Lord to the glory of God the Father." The name of Jesus is above every name—above the name of every individual, above the name of every sickness and disease. Jesus is above all.

We pray to the Father in the name of Jesus because that is where we find authority. God chose to give authority to Jesus. We have to believe Jesus has authority. When we do, Jesus said we could ask anything in His name and He would do it (John 14:14). When we believe, then we will see Jesus clearly as having all authority in heaven and earth. Since He has such authority, He can make other things clear to us too.

The more we believe in the authority, the more we're able to receive the rewards, the blessings, the life, the love, the revelation, the answers to prayer, the miracles, the breakthroughs in finances and in the mind and in the spirit. The more we see He's all authority, the more it makes things possible. It makes the impossible, possible.

We all need the impossible to become possible at times in our lives. Jesus needed the impossible to become possible for Him. When He died at Calvary, things looked bleak and hopeless. To the disciples it looked as if all their hopes were hanging on the cross. But, three days later, just as He had said, God resurrected Him from the dead and with this glorious resurrection God had made the impossible possible.

Submit to the Authority

Jesus said, "All power is given to me in heaven and in earth" (Matthew 28:18). He also said, "Behold, I give unto you power" (Luke 10:19). Why don't we see this power (which means authority) in the Body of Christ today? It is because people aren't reading the Word and seeing Jesus and His authority clearly. The more we believe it, the more we will see it.

It's searching the Word to help us believe what God has said. It's believing we're under authority in Him. It's doing His Word, which is a part of His authority. It's praising and worshiping Him and going on to know more and more of God's truth. It's stepping out in faith, believing that truth, and then seeing its results.

We have to see Jesus clearer in every area. When we read the gospels and the letters in the New Testament, it brings us more understanding and knowledge about Jesus. The more we know about Him, the more we will believe in Him. And the more we believe in Him, the more we will see Him. We need to be like the Bereans to whom Paul ministered in Acts. The Bible says, "They received the word with all readiness of mind, and searched the scriptures daily, whether those things were so" (Acts 17:11).

Trusting His Voice

When an airplane is traveling through a thick blanket of clouds or fog, how do the pilots see where they are going or know how to land under these conditions? They rely on radar. Pilots have to trust what they read on the radar and what the voice from the control tower is telling them.

Pilots are trained to trust their radar even above their own instincts because their inner ear can play tricks on them. They have learned to have confidence in the voice coming to them from the control tower. They may not even know that particular air traffic controller, but they trust his voice.

The people who are traveling on the plane have to trust the pilot, whom they don't know, and trust the voice coming over the airplane's intercom system. Believe me, when you can't see a thing outside the plane windows or the lightning is cracking around you or the turbulence is shaking the plane as if it were a toy, you learn what trust is.

You have to trust the pilot. There's nothing else you can do. You can't bail out. You have to trust that voice and try to be still and not panic. Every time you board a plane you are trusting and believing in the pilot and all the other flight personnel long before you see the results of a safe landing.

We can't see God, but we can trust His voice. He will take us through the storms and the fog and all the other times when it is hard to see. When we put our trust in Him, believing what He has told us, then it won't be long until we will be able to see. Believing comes first, then we will see more of Jesus and what He can do for us.

Chapter 5

Focused Upon Jesus

Seeing the Beauty

I first taught on "Seeing Jesus More Clearly," while I was ministering in Austria. The lodge, where I stayed in Pertisau, was nestled in a valley with the impressive peaks of the Austrian Alps rising around it. The scenery was magnificent and I took dozens of pictures. Many of the people who lived there paid little attention to the scenery around them. It was such a common sight to them, they forgot to enjoy it. They had stopped seeing the beauty right before their eyes.

We who live in less glamorous places than the Austrian Alps might think we would never take such beauty for granted. Surely, if we were privileged to live in the shadow of such magnificant mountains, we would not forget to look up and appreciate their majesty. In reality, we are all prone to take the beauty around us for granted, not only our physical surroundings, but also in our spiritual life. We don't see what lies right in front of us. We need to be reminded now and then to look up and see Jesus.

We must remember to concentrate on Jesus or we will begin to take Him and His majesty for granted. Our vision becomes dimmed, our sense of excitement in knowing Jesus and serving Him becomes dulled. We stop appreciating what we have as children of God, and we no longer see His benefits.

This happened with the children of Israel, as they traveled through the wilderness toward the promised land. They often murmured and complained, forgetting what God had done for them. At one point, God sent poisonous serpents into their camp as punishment for their complaints. In fear of their life they turned to Moses for help.

The Lord told Moses to fashion a brass serpent and place it upon a pole. Anyone who was bitten by one of the poisonous snakes would only have to look up at this brass serpent to be healed. Numbers 21:9 says, "If a serpent had bitten any man, when he beheld the serpent of brass, he lived." The brass serpent had no power in itself. It was simply a visual aid to help the people focus their faith for healing.

Jesus used that same visual aid to reveal His purpose for coming to earth. As He talked with Nicodemus, Jesus said, "As Moses lifted up the serpent in the wilderness, even so must the Son of man be lifted up" (John 3:14). Such a visual aid makes an impression upon our heart and mind. We teach children with pictures because that helps them understand and remember the lesson. Jesus gave us this picture of Himself so we might remember to look to the Lord for what we need.

Psalm 103:2 says, "Bless the Lord, O my soul, and forget not all his benefits." What are the benefits of serving Jesus? The benefits include healing, forgiveness, miracles, love, peace, joy, strength, and many other things. Psalm 68:19 tells us God "daily loadeth us with benefits." The blessings of God are too numerous to count.

But we have to be reminded of this, because sometimes all the difficulties we face in life cover up the blessings. They dull the shine of life; they wear us down and cause us to forget how fortunate we are. Sometimes we see only clouds and not sunshine. We don't remember all the benefits that come from serving God.

This is what hinders people much of the time. We see the big problems facing us and we forget to thank the Lord for what He has already done for us. We don't see God as the answer and then we complain and doubt because an answer doesn't come. We must focus on God instead of on the problems. We must remember to count our blessings.

God sends His blessings and benefits to draw us closer to Him, to His Word, to prayer, to praise, and to worship. He wants to show us He is real, He is true, He cares about everything in our lives, and He wants to help us. He wants us to keep our eyes focused upon Him.

It is amazing how often we receive miracles and blessings from God and then just walk away from Him. We don't go to church, we don't read the Word, we don't praise the Lord. We let the cares of life pull us away from God and we stop seeing the beauty of Jesus.

If we're honest, we all have to admit we're guilty of taking things for granted. We forget to be grateful for good health or a good job, for loved ones, for beauty around us, for the grace of God, and His goodness. If we take these things for granted, after a while, we simply stop seeing them—until they are threatened or altogether gone.

What causes us to take God for granted, to grow dull in spirit, to lose sight of Jesus? There are any number of reasons. The natural circumstances of day-to-day living can simply wear us down. Difficulties, trials, and problems discourage us and make us doubt God's goodness. Fear and other negative emotions drive away courage and joy and cause us to pull back from life. Of course, the devil works to steal our vision and stop our progress. It's his aim to try to get people to stop serving God.

Jesus spoke of this in a parable He told about a farmer planting seeds in Mark 4:3-8. Some of the seeds fell on the wayside. This was the unpaved road that ran alongside the field. Thousands of feet passing over the road had made it hard. The seeds that fell could not penetrate the soil and the birds came and ate them.

Some seeds fell on rocky soil and they quickly grew, but without a root system, the plants quickly died. Other seeds fell among thorns and were choked out. Only the seeds that fell on good ground actually yielded any fruit.

The seed represents the Word of God. When the Word falls upon a heart hardened by time and life, it doesn't always penetrate to the core. Satan can quickly steal it away.

What is the solution to a heart grown tired and worn and hard? The answer is to be revived and awakened. We need to have our vision sharpened and focused, once again. First Corinthians 15:34

tells us to "awake to righteousness." To awake means to rouse from sleep or inactivity, to step up, to become active or aware. There are many people in the Body of Christ who need a reawakening.

The Psalmist wrote, "Though I walk in the midst of trouble, thou wilt revive me" (Psalm 138:7). The Lord is interested in seeing us awakened and stirred and serving Him to the best of our ability. He wants us to see Him clearly through the seed of His Word planted in our heart.

Hosea 10:12 tells us to "break up your fallow ground: for it is time to seek the Lord, till he come and rain righteousness upon you." To break up the ground means to plow it and prepare it to receive the seed. We have to prepare our heart to receive the Word. We "break up the ground" of our heart through humility and repentance.

Going Forward

When the Lord gives us insight or revelation from His Word, the devil will come immediately to try to take that word. He's going to try to talk us out of it and discourage us from believing it. We can receive miracles of healing and deliverance, yet later we can drift away from believing in miracles and healing. The devil steals it away. We no longer see Jesus as the healer.

Many people drift away from the answers. Though we may have seen the spiritual things of

God clearly at one time, we gradually move away from it. Instead of progressing in faith, we sit still, doing nothing, or we slide backward to doubt and dullness of spirit.

Goethe, the German philosopher, said, "He who doesn't go forward goes backward." That's true in our spiritual life. We can never let our guard down as far as protecting our salvation or our standing with God. There is a real enemy who would like nothing better than to destroy our progress.

In everything Jesus does, He's challenged people to follow Him. He is always moving forward. He wants us to be like Him—to be loving, to be forgiving, to give, to pray.

Many people don't want to go forward and follow Jesus in the basic things of loving or forgiving someone. If we aren't going forward, we are losing our vision of Jesus. If we stop seeing Jesus, we won't have anything to focus on as we walk down the path behind Him.

In churches, year after year, we are not making progress in our Christian walk. We have become insensitive to the Holy Spirit and seem oblivious to what is going on in the spiritual realm. We have grown cold in our love for the Lord and we no longer see Jesus clearly. We are drifting, even though we have the answers to life in the Word of God. The

Bible says not only to be hearers of the Word, but to be doers of the Word (James 1:22). That is the key to keeping focused on Jesus and preventing a dull spirit and mind.

Most of Jesus' disciples stopped following Him. John 6:66 says, "From that time many of His disciples went back, and walked no more with Him." These disciples drifted away from the truth and reality of Jesus.

Jesus turned to the twelve disciples and asked them, "Will ye also go away?" Peter answered Him, "Lord, to whom shall we go? Thou hast the words of eternal life" (John 6:67,68).

As I've ministered in churches over the years, I've seen the same problem. The people are not advancing, because they're not seeing Jesus, they're not studying the Word, they're not walking in it, they don't want to make changes. We are praying for revival, but to get revival we have to *do* something.

A person must be willing to change before change will occur. There must be a desire to get tuned up and running at optimum condition. We must determine to chart our course rather than drift through life. Only then will we be able to see Jesus and His kingdom. Only then will we find our place in serving Him.

It is no disgrace to admit the need for a spiritual tune up. We tune up our cars, lawnmowers and a multitude of mechanical things. I had to take my car to the shop not long ago, because the engine was making too much noise, and it wasn't running smoothly. The valves needed a precision adjustment, so it would work the way it was meant to work.

Many of us need a fine tuning. Adjustments need to be made so we can function the way God means for us to function in the Body of Christ. Everyone needs to be fine tuned now and then. Without the constant adjustments and fine tuning we need, we will wander aimlessly through our Christian life. God doesn't want us to be sitting still, accomplishing nothing in life. He wants us moving on in Him all the time. He wants us to see Him and participate in all His majesty and glory.

The Eyes Grow Dim

Failing eyesight is sometimes the natural process of eyes that grow old. It can also develop when someone does not properly care for his eyes. In First Samuel we read of a priest in the days of the judges whose eyes "began to wax dim, that he could not see" (I Samuel 3:2). His name was Eli.

Eli's failing sight was a physical condition brought on by his advanced age, but Eli had let his spiritual eyes grow dim as well. He was aware of the corruption in his two sons, who also served as priests, but he only made half-hearted attempts to stop their perversion. Eli could not see clearly and his actions betrayed his spiritual condition.

Samuel grew up in Eli's care and God anointed him to fill the office of prophet and priest. When he was young, Samuel did not recognize the voice of God, but as time passed he learned to listen. He developed a strong relationship with the Lord, paying heed to His words so that "none fell to the ground." Samuel walked with God all of his life, yet his sons, like Eli's, did not follow the way of the Lord. Every individual must establish a relationship with God and maintain it day in and day out.

Keep Focused

The key to a strong, successful Christian life is to see clearly all the time. In the natural, we keep our eyes clear by using eyedrops, changing the prescription on glasses, taking contacts out and giving our eyes a rest, and not straining our eyes. We all work to insure that our eyes stay as healthy and clear as possible. We should work equally hard at keeping our spiritual eyes clear.

Many people have never learned to see clearly. We let negative thinking and the wrong voices influence us and hinder our ability to see. Sometimes it seems like we are lost in a fog.

When I was ministering in England, I learned how dangerous fog can be. On those evenings when the fog was thick I had to concentrate completely when I was driving. I could see no more than two or three feet in front of me. I wasn't going to go 70 miles an hour down the road when the fog was so thick I couldn't see the lights of the other cars on the road. I had to concentrate and drive cautiously in the fog.

We should concentrate to get the right guidance from the Lord and we should be cautious when we're in the fog spiritually. We have to be willing to pray, "Lord, open my eyes, I want to see Jesus." We should be determined to see God.

Traditions of Men

When people sit on church pews and fail to absorb anything from the Word, the ministry, or the moving of the Holy Spirit, then their hearts are likely to become hard and dry like an old piece of bread. We think we know everything there is to know and we've seen everything there is to see and we don't learn anything new.

The Pharisees of Jesus' day were hardened by their rigid adherence to their traditions and doctrines. Jesus came preaching something new and different, but they didn't want to hear it. They didn't want to see the grace and truth He brought. A rigid, narrow, or wrong doctrine can keep us from seeing Jesus.

We can't let ourselves get so familiar with the great truths of the Bible that we no longer see how wonderful they are. And we can't let the many false teachings and false doctrines circulating these days keep us from seeing clearly that only Jesus is the way, the truth, and the life.

The Bible has much to say about staying away from bad teaching. Ephesians 4:14 tells us to "be no more children, tossed to and fro, and carried about with every wind of doctrine." Yet there are many people who are carried here and there by every new idea or teaching that comes along. This happens because they are not rooted in the Word of God. Ephesians 5:6 tells us to "let no man deceive you with vain words: for because of these things cometh the wrath of God upon the children of disobedience." When we're not seeing clearly and discerning truth, we can be deceived.

A few years ago a man predicted the Lord was going to come back in 1988. When He didn't come that year, the man predicted He would return in 1989. Many people were deceived by this man in 1988 and then continued to believe the same deception in 1989!

We can be deceived by these things and then we start judging everyone—even those who are preaching the truth—because we were hurt by a lie. The truth becomes evil to us and we don't receive the Word. Then we fall more and more into darkness.

We are not going to see the Word or the truth when we are lost in deception and are emotionally damaged.

If we follow what the Word says and listen to people who know what they are talking about, we will be able to sift through false doctrines. Colossians 2:8 says, "Beware lest any man spoil you through philosophy and vain deceit, after the traditions of men, after the rudiments of the world, and not after Christ."

The Pharisees and Sadducees didn't want to accept Jesus or His teaching. They had their own teaching, and the message Jesus brought didn't fit into their neat package of ideas about God. They didn't want to change and so they chose not to see the truth Jesus spoke.

The Pharisees and Sadducees knew the law very well. Jesus said they had the key to knowledge yet "ye entered not in yourselves, and them that were entering in ye hindered" (Luke 11:52). They wanted to keep the people in bondage. Jesus wanted to set people free and in setting them free He exposed their teaching as wrong.

Ask the Lord

We have to open our heart and mind every day, when we're reading the Word and when we listen to good teaching, so we will receive the Word. Even though we might not understand everything we read or hear at first, if it is based on the Word of God, we can still receive it by faith. The Holy Spirit will give us understanding in time.

Read this as a prayer to the Lord:

> "Father God, I don't want to have hardness of heart. I give You the opportunity and the freedom to work in my heart, to take hardness of heart from me so I can see Jesus and the kingdom of God more clearly. I want a pliable heart. In Jesus name, amen."

Today, many people hold on to the belief that Jesus doesn't heal. They say healing passed away with the apostles. That's why they can't see Jesus clearly as the healer and they don't receive the healing they need. They've chosen to believe a doctrine of men instead of the Word of God.

God broke through the darkness in my life with the light of the gospel to bring me to Him. I was raised in a Jewish home, but even when I was going to Hebrew school, I didn't believe in Judaism. When I left Hebrew school, I didn't hold on to Judaism.

I believe that is one of the reasons the Lord was able to draw me to Him. I had no doctrine standing in the way of God's voice. It's harder to unlearn things and get reprogrammed to learn new things when we're holding on to bad teachings. The more we hold on to a bad doctrine, the more we're going to be unhappy in life, the more frustrated we're going to be, and the more we're going to struggle.

After my bar mitzvah at age thirteen, I let go of everything having to do with religion. I was empty of religion and several years later, when I started my search for God, I was totally ignorant of spiritual matters. I found the Bible the rabbis had given me at my bar mitzvah and said, "God, I don't know where You are, but I'm going to find You. I want to know the truth."

We must want to see, but that isn't enough. We also need to ask God to show Himself, to show us the truth. If we can't see, then we can ask God to help us see clearly and give us the desire to see Him as He is. We must want to see Him as our way, truth, and life no matter where we are.

As I taught on seeing Jesus, I told the people in Austria about the song we sing in America, "Open my eyes, Lord, I want to see Jesus." I asked them to use that as a prayer every day.

If we're not seeing clearly we can ask the Lord, "Help me see clearly." Philip said to Jesus in the Upper Room, "Lord, show us the Father" (John 14:8). When I was searching for God, I prayed, "Lord, show me the truth about Jesus."

We have beauty right before our eyes with the Word and with Jesus. We don't want to miss any of that beauty because we have grown dull in spirit or have let our religion become more important than our Lord. Ask the Lord to keep your eyes open and focused upon Jesus. Pray as the Psalmist David, “Open Thou mine eyes, that I may behold wondrous things” (Psalm 119:18).

Chapter 6

Religion or Reality

Lost in a Fog

When a London fog rolls in from the sea, everything takes on a different look. Shapes and shadows can become distorted. All the familiar landmarks are changed and sometimes completely disappear. It's easy to become lost in a London fog.

We often read of accidents taking place because of fog. Actually, the fog is not the only cause for the accident. Equally at fault is the judgment of the people who failed to realize the danger of not taking the effects of the fog on their senses, especially their vision. At a time when they should have exercised caution, they chose to ignore the circumstances and the result was disastrous.

Religious pride can be a "fog" that keeps people from seeing clearly and results in disastrous living. We should concentrate to get the right guidance from the Lord and we should be cautious when we're in a spiritual fog. We have to be willing to pray, "Lord, open my eyes, I want to see Jesus." We should be determined to see God.

Many people have never learned to see clearly. We let negative thinking and the wrong voices influence us and hinder our ability to see. Sometimes it seems like we are lost in a fog. Often as Christians, we let religious spirits distort our vision and our thinking. We can't see Jesus because we let wrong ideas about Him cloud our mind. As with a London fog, the beautiful castles, beautiful rivers, and beautiful manors can be there, but we can't see them because they are shrouded in that fog.

Our religious beliefs will affect our spiritual vision. I've heard people outside the Church say, "Jesus was a good teacher, but we don't believe His teachings." Though we Christians don't come right out and say that, often we live as if it were true.

If Jesus was a good teacher, then He must have said something important, something worth listening to, something worth believing. For many people, Jesus was a good teacher, yet they don't want to do what He said. They don't want to see

Him as He truly is. Today, many people are like the Pharisees of long ago. They will say Jesus was a good teacher and prophet, but they don't take it past that because their religious beliefs stand in the way. They want to intellectualize everything instead of accepting Jesus by faith.

Too often in the Body of Christ people know *about* Jesus, but don't *know* Jesus. We haven't taken the time to get to know Him, to establish a relationship with Him, and to enjoy His fellowship on a day-to-day basis. We think we know who He is, but we don't see Him as He is.

Perhaps the source of the problem is the religious teaching we have received over the years. If we're taught things about Jesus that aren't biblically correct, we're not going to see Him clearly.

This doesn't always have to do with official church doctrine either. Much of what we learn in church about Jesus or God comes in an informal way. What our teachers and preachers say about God makes an impression upon us even when we don't think we're paying attention. Over the years these impressions add up to give us our image of God.

For example, if you grew up in church, you may have heard things in Sunday School such as, "God won't love you if you're bad" or "Maybe if you're real good God will heal you or bring you a puppy or help you make an 'A' in science." Probably, without being aware of what they are doing, such teachers are presenting ideas about God that aren't scriptural. Yet they stay in our mind, and like a fog, distort our image of God.

We will not see clearly if we don't study the Word until we get clarity. People get in trouble when they hear a little bit of Scripture, a partial teaching, a preacher's or teacher's opinion and run with it. No one is more dogmatic than a person who thinks he knows what the Bible says but really doesn't.

The words we speak reflect what we see most of the time. But, if people are seeing wrong, they will say the wrong words, and then they will receive the wrong results. We say what we *see* and we receive what we *say*.

If we see God as a stern judge who delights in inflicting pain and suffering on helpless human beings, then our words will reflect that. If we see God as our big Buddy in the sky ready to fulfill our every whim, then we will talk that way. Both images are wrong because they are too narrow and unscriptural. But, there are many Christians convinced by their own religiosity that their image is the right one.

Black or Blue

Kansas City sport fans had a love/hate relationship with superstar Bo Jackson when he played baseball for the Kansas City Royals. When Jackson stepped out on the field wearing a Kansas City Royals uniform, he was greeted with applause and cheers, but when he went to Kansas City wearing a Los Angeles Raiders uniform to play against the Kansas City Chiefs, what he heard were boos and jeers. When Bo was in Royal blue, he was seen as a hero. When he wore Raider black, he was seen as a villain. This can happen spiritually too. We form prejudices against God and against other people based upon our distorted beliefs and narrow vision.

I heard from a friend about a certain minister who was a good teacher, but my friend wouldn't walk across the street to hear him speak. Yet, that's exactly what he needs. He needs to walk across the street and hear him and repent and get delivered from his negative attitude. If he can't see his brother clearly, he will never see Jesus clearly with such narrow thinking.

I enjoyed the story told in the movie, *Dances With Wolves*. Lt. John Dunbar was stationed at a remote outpost on the American plains. At first he and his Lakota Sioux neighbors were suspicious and hostile toward one another. To Dunbar, the Indians are not-very-successful horse thieves. To the

Lakota, Dunbar was "a puny white man with a smart horse." But, in time the Lakotas and Dunbar became friends and allies and, eventually, family. A lasting relationship developed as they changed their narrow views and saw each other as they really were.

Our view of Jesus may not come close to the reality of Jesus. It depends upon what our perspective is. Our religious beliefs play an important role in determining how we see God. We are guilty sometimes of creating God in our own image or ideas.

Isaiah wrote about a person who cuts down a tree and uses part of the wood for a fire and the other part to carve an idol. He fashions a god to suit his own idea yet he is blinded to the true God. Of such people Isaiah said, "They have not known nor understood: for he hath shut their eyes, that they cannot see; and their hearts, that they cannot understand" (Isaiah 44:18).

The best and most accurate way to see is from God's point of view. The Word of God will show us not only how to see Jesus, but also how to see ourselves and our brothers and sisters. Some of the ways God sees us is saved, healed, prosperous, righteous, and called.

I use healing as an example so often because God called me to be a healing evangelist. He spoke to me shortly after I was saved and told me everywhere I went in the world there would be healings and miracles. I didn't know anything about healing. It wasn't something I learned in Hebrew school. I accepted what God said to me with childlike faith. I had no doctrinal teaching to turn me against the God-given concept that healing is available to God's children today.

If we are confused about God and in darkness because we put away good scriptures, we may miss out on many of God's promises and blessings. We may know Jesus is the Light of the world, but He can't illuminate us because there is no Word in us.

God is not the author of confusion, but of peace (I Corinthians 14:33). The devil brings confusion to people's minds. When something is not clear in our mind and it's getting more confused and our mind is swimming in a fog, we need to rebuke that. Confusion about the Word doesn't come from God. God brings clarity and peace.

Jesus speaks clearly to us and His words are words of peace, strength, love, and joy. When anything comes to our mind speaking contrary to this, it's not from God. We know God is love, joy, peace, and strength.

When something says we can't have what God offers, this advice is not from God. That's why we must read the Word in its entirety. We need to know what it says personally. Jesus wants to have a relationship with every individual who will receive Him. He will reveal Himself to us as we read the Word with a soft, pliable heart and an open mind.

The devil likes to discourage us and confuse us about God. When we get up in the morning, he tries to bring confusion to our mind. That's why it's important to start our mornings with prayer, praise to God, and Bible reading. Throughout the day, we can listen to good music tapes or the Word, and put Scripture cards around the house or on our desk. When we keep the Word of God strong in our mind, then the devil won't be able to confuse us with his lies.

Blinded Eyes

The devil works to blind our spiritual eyes. He wants to take all the glory he can from God. He wants to shut people's mouths from giving God the glory. He wants to discourage us so we won't praise God or give testimony. But, the more we declare what God has done for us, the more clear Jesus will be to us.

The Bible says in Revelation 12:11 that we overcome the devil by the blood of the Lamb and the word of our testimony. There is power in a positive testimony about God's goodness. The blind man described in John, chapter 9, gave a good testimony about Jesus and it helped him to see spiritually as well as physically. The disciples were concerned about the man's sin, but Jesus was concerned about the man's need. Jesus proclaimed to the man, "I am the light of the world." Jesus anointed this blind man by putting a mixture of spittle and clay on his face and then He told him to go to the pool of Siloam and wash.

This blind man had to walk across the city, perhaps bumping into things along the way. Being obedient to Jesus' words wasn't easy for him. He may have walked into walls and bumped into people on his way. He could have stumbled over obstacles in the narrow streets. He might have had to work his way through the confusion of the marketplace with its masses of people and animals and its sounds and smells.

How much did the blind man want to see? How much do people want to see today? There's a price to pay if we want to see clearly. We need to study the Word and lose our religious pride. If what the Bible teaches goes against our doctrine, we need to change our belief and believe what the Bible says. If what Jesus tell us to do is unusual or difficult, we must be willing to make the effort.

The blind man wanted to see and he was willing to do whatever was necessary to gain his sight. His friends and neighbors questioned his new ability to see. It never entered the minds of these people the blind man might receive a miracle. They thought he would be sitting by the road, blind and begging, for the rest of his life.

They took the man to the authorities. Everyone should have been rejoicing because the man was not blind any more. Instead they were complaining because it didn't go along with their doctrine of healing on the Sabbath.

Whenever miracles or dramatic healing is taking place, there will be divisions among the people. It ruffles their religious feathers because they can't explain what is happening. The Pharisees didn't believe because they had hardness of heart, rebellion, religious spirits, strife, and many other negative things working in their hearts. They couldn't see a miracle because they were only looking for legalities.

When they questioned the man about Jesus, he said that Jesus was a prophet. This was the first step in opening his spiritual eyes. In an effort to explain the miracle they tried to attack Jesus' character, calling Jesus a sinner. The man answered "Whether He be a sinner or no, I know not: one thing I know, that, whereas I was blind, now I see. Then said they to him again, What did He to thee? how opened He thine eyes? He answered, I have told you already, and ye did not hear" (John 9:25-27).

Often the Bible says, "He who has an ear to hear, let him hear." These leaders of the synagogue didn't want to hear. They didn't want to see. They didn't want to have any softness of heart to be open to the miracles of Jesus. A religious mind will always try to reason things away.

Knowing and acting on the truth sets us free. That's why Jesus was such a threat to the leaders of His day and even to many leaders in this day and age. Jesus is truth. Those who follow Him and hear His voice will be free from the legalism of religious tradition. We will see Jesus clearly.

The blind man's physical eyes were opened first. Then his spiritual eyes were opened. The Pharisees had physical eyes to see, but their hearts were hardened by religious spirits and wrong attitudes. They were blinded because the Light of the world was right there and they couldn't see Him. They wanted to hold onto their religious spirits. They wanted to stay in pride and other bad attitudes. But the man who received that miracle had a heart to praise God and give God the glory.

Finally, the Pharisees said to Jesus, "Are we blind also? Jesus said unto them, If ye were blind, ye should have no sin: but now ye say, We see; therefore your sin remaineth" (John 9:40-41).

He was saying, "You say you see, but that is only your religious spirit and pride. You don't really see. I'm the Son of God, and you don't see Me. I did a miracle for this blind man, but you couldn't praise God for the miracle."

Religious spirits kept the Pharisees from seeing Jesus. That's why they were so critical of Jesus for healing on the sabbath. It went against their tradition and their understanding of the law. Keeping the law was more important than helping people. No wonder they couldn't see Jesus clearly. Helping people was why He came.

The Pharisees and other religious leaders were always pointing back to Moses and Abraham to justify their stand against Jesus. They were trying so hard to be religious they failed to see reality. They knew the Scriptures very well, but not well enough to see Jesus in the Scriptures.

Chapter 7

The Lamp and Light of the Word

The Light of the Word

How do we see Jesus more clearly? If we wish to look beyond religious teaching, we must study the Word of God. The Word brings clarity and truth. The Word shows us Jesus, as God has revealed Him through the Scriptures from Genesis to Revelation.

The Holy Spirit inspired the writing of the 66 books of the Bible through 42 different men, over a 1600-year period. The Holy Spirit is the author of the Bible and we have the Holy Spirit here today to help us see what God wants us to know about Himself. As we study the Word with an open heart we will find a clear picture of Jesus. He brings the healing, miracles, joy and the love.

God wants us to read His Word for ourselves. The Word of God brings clarity about all of life as the Holy Spirit teaches us and guides us through its pages. In Ephesians 1:16-18, Paul prays for us that we might be given the spirit of wisdom and revelation in the knowledge of Him; that our eyes might be enlightened through understanding; and, that we might know His hope for our calling and the glorious riches of His provision for us through our inheritance as His sons and daughters.

The more we read the Bible, attend church services, and learn about Jesus, the stronger our faith gets and the more we start seeing who Jesus is in every area. According to His Word, He commanded the light to shine out of darkness and into our heart so we might receive the light of the knowledge of the glory of God in the face of Jesus Christ (II Corinthians 4:6).

God wants the light of the Word in our heart and mind. We can have that light by hiding the Word in our heart and by renewing our mind. The mind is renewed when the light of the Word enters in. We want light in our mind so we can see.

The more we walk in the light of what we know, the more we are going to see how good God is to us.

We will see what He has provided for us through the Word. We will have a more thankful heart and will know God cares about us. Because we are not continually walking in the light of His Word, we don't think God cares.

The entrance of the Word of God into our heart and mind gives us light, which brings understanding to the simple (Psalm 119:130). It shows us Jesus in all His greatness, as we have an open heart to learn. Yet, most of us find it hard to admit we are simple and need understanding. We all, sometimes, struggle with the same things that hindered the Pharisees. We let pride or fear stand in our way of seeing Jesus.

Many people put up resistance to the Word, to the truth and to God's way. When we put up resistance in our heart and mind, there is no entrance for light. The only way to get light in our heart and mind is to receive the Word. Jesus said that He is the Light of the world and that His Word is light. This light represents knowledge and understanding. We need knowledge to function successfully in life.

The Hidden Word

We must hide God's Word in our heart. Psalm 119:11 says, "Thy word have I hid in mine heart, that I might not sin against thee." When we have the Word inside us, it is not so easily lost in the midst of difficult times. We are not so likely to be misled by false teachings when we have an intimate and personal knowledge of the Word.

Did you ever watch an old western on television? Remember when the cowboys were out on the open range and they heated the branding iron to brand the cattle? They still do that today. That's what God wants to do with the Word. He wants the Word permanently imprinted upon our heart. The light that Word gives us will enable us to keep seeing Jesus clearly.

The Lighted Path

Psalm 119:105 says, "Thy word is a lamp unto my feet, and a light unto my path." One of the biggest problems everyone has in life is in knowing what path to take; what decisions we need to make. The Word of God will guide us and help us make the right choice.

In the days when lamps or lanterns were used, the light had to be held close to the ground when people were out at night. The light from the lamp would illuminate the place for each step, one step at a time. The Word of God is like that too. It shows us how to walk through the darkness of this world, revealing one step at a time.

It's so important that we learn to get in tune with God, to learn His Word, and to know when He is talking to us. God always tells us the truth.

That's why we need an open heart and mind at all times. Only then will we see clearly.

I usually travel by plane in my ministry and have flown in all kinds of weather. When I'm on a plane, I'm praying for the pilot, and for the angels to be around the plane to keep it safe. Sometimes when we're coming down from 39,000 feet through the clouds, we can't see anything.

When I flew to Jersey Island in the English Channel, we were coming in for the first time and it was too foggy to land. We couldn't see anything. The fog was too low for us to land because it was an island. We had to wait for the fog to be higher. The pilot said, "We're going to circle around one time. If the fog hasn't lifted, we'll go back to London."

As we circled the island—it took about a half hour—I was praying the entire time, "Lord, please lift the clouds and the fog so we can land." So we came around again and by the time we did, my prayer was answered, the fog had lifted and we were able to land safely.

Sometimes we have to pray, "Lord, lift the fog off me. Lift the bad clouds off me so I can see." Seeing God's way clearly is a constant battle. We go through warfare nearly every day. Something happens to bring disappointment and it might obscure our vision. The devil comes against the natural mind to steal the vision from us.

The more Word we put in our heart, the more the Lord can light our lives. Jesus is the Light of the world, but let's make Him more personal. Let's make Him the light of our lives, our clarity, and our thinking, the light unto our path.

Chapter 8

An Open Heart

Under the Influence

Every day we are influenced by many things and many people. These influences, by someone or something, have either a negative or positive effect. They originate with family or friends, bosses or teachers, neighbors and associates, church and community leaders. We should also include the media, sports or entertainment figures, social, political and economic conditions, or educational opportunities. It might be gender or race or national origin or family upbringing. All of these people and circumstances can play a role in our lives. They influence the way we think, the way we act and the way we view life. The effect continues throughout our lifetime.

Without being aware of it, we might be letting these influences determine the way we see Jesus. Very often our view of God, as our heavenly Father, may depend upon what kind of earthly father we have. Our concept of Jesus may be strongly influenced by the teaching we received at home and at church when we were small children. If that teaching conflicts with what we are learning as adults, or if it doesn't line up with the Word of God, it may hinder us from seeing Jesus clearly now.

So, we must weed out the bad influences in our lives. Sometimes it is necessary to get away from friends or counselors who are bad for us and seek those who will be a positive influence. We don't want bad influences to cause confusion in our mind, or worse, to close our mind to God's truth.

Most movie stars and professional athletes will hire agents to help promote and advance their careers. They want to find an agent who will give them good advice and will have their best interest in mind. If that agent doesn't help them, they'll soon be looking for a new agent.

They may sound a little cold-blooded or self-serving and, in some cases, this may be true. But, the principle behind such advisors is a sound one. A good counsellor can prevent us from accepting influences that will hurt us or hinder us or mislead us. To succeed as a Christian, we shouldn't accept those influences that would keep us from seeing Jesus clearly, because they don't come from God.

Depression or discouragement is not from God. If something is creating worry, fear, doubt or confusion, we don't have to accept it, because it did not originate from God.

If a delivery man knocked on your door and handed you a big box tied up with a bright ribbon, you'd say, "Oh, a present for me!" Then you'd ask the man, "What is it?" Suppose his answer was "Forty-two rattlesnakes. Sign here; it's all yours."

Are you going to sign for 42 rattlesnakes? Not unless you're a zookeeper. You don't need 42 rattlesnakes slithering around your house. You surely wouldn't get any sleep at night! But, that's exactly what many of us do. We sign for the doubt, fear, worry, cares and everything else that people and circumstances and the devil hand us and we don't get much sleep.

The devil tries to get us to sign for the negatives by believing the thoughts he brings to our mind. If you have ten million dollars in your bank account and a voice comes to your mind and says, "You don't have enough money to even buy a hamburger," are you going to believe that thought? No!

If you have a relationship with the great and mighty God of the universe and a thought comes that says, "You aren't going to make it in life," are you going to believe that thought? Well...The answer should be "no" in this case too, but often it isn't. Why are we so quick to believe the devil's lies about God?

If a thought says Jesus is not our healer, we don't have to believe that thought. If something says our needs will not be met, we take what God says, rather than what the thought says. The Bible says, "My God shall supply all your needs" (Philippians 4:19). The devil does not want us to believe God's provision through Jesus. He wants to undermine us so we don't see Jesus or His truth, so we don't see His answers, so we don't see that life can be successful and happy for us.

The devil's objective is to steal the Word. Our objective is to make sure he doesn't. The Word helps us see Jesus more clearly. The Word gives us guidance in life as a lamp unto our feet and a light unto our path (Psalm 119:105).

It's so important to see Jesus as He is in many different areas, because when we see Him as He is—as our Savior, healer, wisdom, peace, strength, and friend—then we're able to receive what we see Him as. If we let outside influences close our mind to Jesus, we won't be able to see Him and we won't receive what we need from Him.

Within the Body of Christ, many are confused about Jesus. We don't see Jesus clearly and we don't understand what He is saying to us through His Word. God's love, expressed through Jesus and the Word, is simple. We complicate it by our mind, hardness of heart, rebellion, and religious spirits. God wants us to see things clearly. If we don't see Jesus clearly, we're not going to understand life the way He wants us to understand it.

No matter what's going on with us emotionally, God is not the one who complicates matters in our lives. Betty Malz wrote, "When life gets complicated, it's not of God—because He moves in simple, elegant ways to achieve His purposes." God doesn't make things difficult for us. We do that ourselves by not obeying what He says.

The Bible tells us to resist the devil and he will flee (James 4:7). If we don't resist the devil, he's going to do his best to create problems for us. He will bring as much frustration and confusion and fear as we will let him bring. But, if we rebuke the devil and take our authority over him, we'll have victory because that's what the Word says.

Nowhere in the Bible does it say God takes peace away from us. God adds peace because He is peace. The Bible says Jesus gives us peace. If something is trying to take your peace, it's not from God. We can rebuke the devil and not let him take our peace.

In the gospels, Jesus dealt with people in a very simple and direct way. He would ask them what they needed and then He would reach out and meet their need. Jesus didn't make things complicated. He didn't have a list of prerequisites they had to meet before they could receive. His heart's desire is to meet the needs of people.

When we let circumstances, negative thoughts, emotions, and doubting people influence us, we don't see Jesus in this simple, uncomplicated way. This is also when we find it difficult to receive from Jesus. Our mind is cluttered with too many other things. We need to be influenced by God's Word, which will keep us focused on Jesus.

On the Emmaus Road

In Luke 24:13-53 we read about two disciples to whom Jesus ministered as they walked along the road from Jerusalem to Emmaus. At this time, Jesus had already been crucified and had risen from the dead. He came to these two disciples, but they didn't see Jesus. Grief, discouragement, doubt, and fear had closed their minds and their eyes.

Just before Jesus appeared, these two men were talking about what had happened in Jerusalem during the last few days. Jesus, their beloved Master, had been crucified and His body laid in a tomb. Those events were very upsetting and confusing to the disciples.

These men were probably talking about the things Jesus had said concerning His death. Though

He had predicted His death and tried to prepare His disciples for what would happen, they hadn't understood everything He said.

When Jesus came alongside them on the road in His resurrected body, the disciples didn't recognize Him. They had been told Jesus had risen from the dead, but they didn't believe it. They certainly weren't expecting the Lord to join them on their journey.

(If Jesus Christ of Nazareth were to come into many of our churches today, I wonder how many of us would recognize Him. I'm afraid many people wouldn't know it was Jesus because He wouldn't look or act the way we expect Him to.)

Jesus joined them and started a conversation with these two disciples. They were talking about Jesus, but in their minds they had left Him in the grave. The two disciples did not realize their grief was not necessary. So many people today leave Jesus in the grave also. But, He's not there! If we leave Him in the tomb, we are going to miss out on so much because Jesus is not dead. He's alive!

His death had been devastating to the disciples. They had pinned all their hopes and dreams on Jesus, believing He had come to establish a kingdom on earth free from Roman oppression. When He died, their dreams died too.

Cleopas, one of the disciples, treated Jesus as a stranger. He had an insensitive spirit, not as a result of rebellion or stubbornness or pride, but because of confusion and grief. Many people are numbed by the bombardment of the negative and destructive influences around them. Then they become insensitive to what's going on in their life. God wants us to be sensitive to His voice and His leading. He wants us to be aware of the devil's devices. Jesus wants us to know what's happening.

When Jesus questioned them further, they recounted all of the events of the past few days. They knew the rulers crucified Jesus because Jesus said He was the Christ, the Messiah. They had followed this same Jesus of Nazareth and they had seen Him as a prophet. They had experienced His mighty miracles, signs, and wonders, and His words of wisdom, revelation, and His new teachings. But now, as He walked beside them, they failed to recognize Him. He stood before them in more power and glory than ever before and they didn't even see Him.

The same thing is true with many Christians today. We don't sense the Spirit of God when He is present. We should be receptive, like a radar tower. We should receive the good and not the bad. We don't have to receive the lies of the devil and the world.

We feed our spirit and mind, just as we feed our body. Doctors tell us if we take in unhealthy food, then our body will be unhealthy. The same is true of our spirit and our mind. If we feed the unhealthy things of the devil and the world into our soul, it will be unhealthy. If we feed good things into our body, spirit and mind, we'll be strong, alert, and see clearly.

One of the reasons people don't see Jesus is slowness of heart. We aren't sensitive or perceptive. Some of us don't want to believe. We should read the Word and believe what the Word says. It gives us knowledge and strength and victory as we apply that knowledge to our lives.

Jesus began to teach the two disciples as they walked toward Emmaus. He taught them from the books of Moses and the prophets, about Himself. He taught them with authority and great knowledge. Why didn't they ask Him, "Where did You get all this understanding?" Jesus gave the Word to the two men to show them the truth about Himself. But, they still didn't realize it was Jesus.

When they stopped for the night Jesus, the bread of life, fed these disciples with the Word, prophecies, and the teachings. They prepared a meal and as Jesus blessed and broke the bread, their eyes were opened and, at last, they saw Jesus.

Our heart will be moved while we are listening to the Word of God. Those two disciples had been "slow of heart to believe." This is a common problem today too. So many of us have doubts, fears, worries, cares, strife with one another, and many other unhealthy things in our heart. These will prevent the Word from coming in and keep us from seeing Jesus.

When we hear and read the Word, we prepare our hearts to change. That's why we need an open heart for the Word. It's the Word that helps us see Jesus. The scriptures made Jesus clear. That's why, when we preach and teach the Word, so many eyes are opened to see Jesus in each area. When we see Him in each area, we receive what He is in that area. Then we'll understand how to have more victories in life.

If something complicates our mind, we don't have to believe the complication. If something tries to put Jesus out of focus, we don't have to believe that. We don't want to be out of focus as those disciples were.

At the end of their encounter with the risen Christ, the two disciples returned to Jerusalem and found the eleven apostles and the other disciples gathered together. After the group confirmed the resurrection and appearances of Jesus, the two related their experience on the road to Emmaus. As they were speaking, "Jesus himself stood in the midst of them, and saith unto them, Peace be unto you" (Luke 24:36). Even though Jesus stood in their midst and spoke peace to them, they were afraid and thought He was a ghost. A slow heart kept them from believing.

Jesus is the Prince of Peace. He doesn't take peace from us. He gives us peace. Jesus said to them, "Why are you troubled? and why do thoughts arise in your hearts?" (Luke 24:38). He is saying the same to us today, "Why are you troubled? Why are you letting the fears, the cares, and all the anxieties into your heart? Why do wrong thoughts arise in your hearts?" Wherever people were troubled or had a problem and Jesus wanted them to understand something, He said, "Peace be unto you."

Jesus is talking about wrong thinking. The more the "right thoughts" arise in our heart about Him and the Word, the more our faith will grow and become strong. That's why the Bible says, "Keep your heart with all diligence, for out of it flow the issues of life" (Proverbs 4:23).

Jesus tells us many times, "Don't let your heart be troubled." Why do people have heart attacks today? We let fears and cares and worries and anxieties trouble our heart. We put too much pressure on our heart. Jesus gives people the right formula to have a peaceful heart. We must follow the directions Jesus gives us.

Then Jesus said to the disciples who were in the Upper Room, "Behold my hands and my feet, that it is I myself: handle me, and see: for a spirit has not flesh and bones, as you see me have. And when He had thus spoken, He shewed them His hands and His feet," which had the scars from the crucifixion (Luke 24:39). Then, to open their understanding of the scriptures, He spoke of Himself from Moses and the prophets and the Psalms. God wants to open our spiritual eyes. When our spiritual eyes are opened and we walk in the light of what we see, we receive knowledge, understanding, and direction. That builds our faith and then we will see the object of our belief.

At the end of this encounter between Jesus and His disciples, Jesus promised them the gift of the Spirit with power. The Holy Spirit is the author of the Bible. The only way to understand the Bible is through the Holy Spirit opening our eyes. He has to open our eyes so we can understand things and see the truth.

Spirit Guide

The disciples watched Jesus ascend up into heaven, then they went to Jerusalem to wait until they received the power from on high on the day of Pentecost. These people who were afraid and weak, doubtful and timid, had something happen to them. They were changed. They received the Holy Spirit and began to see things clearly.

In reading the Book of Acts, we see great revelation, power and miracles coming forth. The disciples were changed. When they preached, they proclaimed Jesus clearly to people. Some of the apostles were arrested and beaten for preaching about Jesus. The Bible says the magistrates perceived that these men had been with Jesus because of the wisdom and the spirit in them.

The Holy Spirit became their strength, power, and guide. As the disciples followed His leading, they grew in boldness and in understanding. Now they were standing up to the Pharisees and rulers, just as Jesus had done. Now they were preaching with authority and seeing miracles and healing just as Jesus had done. Now they were imitating Christ because they could see Him clearly through the Holy Spirit.

There was a news story not long ago about a father who went to pick up his little girls at school. As they were driving home, he had an allergic reaction to the penicillin he had just taken and lost his vision.

One of the girls began to cry at first, but she controlled her emotions and began to direct her father as he drove. She was able to get him to the hospital. They hit three cars along the way, but very little damage was done and no one was hurt. She saved her father's life.

This brave little girl became his sight, but her father had to be willing to follow her direction. She was his eyes and he followed the directions she spoke to him.

I have found when I'm counseling people, I sometimes have to be their eyes because circumstances and problems may have them blinded. They're confused, they don't know where to go, they don't know what to do, they don't know what decisions to make. They can't see things clearly. A good counselor will hear what people are saying and will be able to give them eyes to see clear thoughts and new hope.

That is what the Holy Spirit does for us. He is our counselor and sometimes He is our eyes. Difficulties come to all of us. We are influenced by circumstances around us all the time. If we are blinded by emotions or fears, we need the Holy Spirit to guide us until we can see for ourselves. He is always available to us.

The head coach of a football team is important, but he needs assistant coaches to help him win a game. He needs the spotters up in the booth, who can see the field better. They have a better vantage point to see what is going on during each play and to spot weaknesses in the opponents formation. They relay the information to the coach, who makes adjustments in his own lineup. Who knows how many games are won and lost because of the people in the booth.

The Holy Spirit takes us to a higher point of view when the circumstances are all we can see. Sometimes we need to make adjustments, based on what the Holy Spirit is telling us, in order to see more clearly. I doubt many of us are so complete and secure in our lives that we don't see the need for some form of improvement. No one has such perfect vision or understanding that they don't need to change and grow.

It's like an eye doctor changing the prescription on a pair of glasses. As a person's eyes change, the glasses have to be adjusted for those changes to keep the vision clear and true. At times, we may find we have lost our focus and are not seeing as clearly as we should in the spiritual realm. We have to make adjustments with the help of the Holy Spirit and the Word of God.

I've had to make adjustments in my life—some large, some small. For example, I never used to like animals. I never had a pet when I was growing up. Then one day I heard a meow at the window of my house. It was a little cat. He went around the house meowing at every window. All those little meows got to me. The little guy was outside asking to come in. I opened the door and let him in and that's how my cat, King, came to live with me.

I had never taken care of an animal before, so I wasn't used to it. I had to make the adjustment.

We all have to make adjustments. The more we make adjustments, the more we see. I made the adjustment and now I see King differently. Before, he was just a cat to me, but now I see he has personality and character.

Opened Eyes

We have to ask God continually to open our eyes to the truth in each area of life. Remember to pray every day, "Open my eyes, Lord. I want to see Jesus."

In Second Kings, chapter 6, we read about the Syrian Army surrounding the little town of Dothan. Elisha, the prophet, was there at the time with his servant and the army had come to capture him. When his servant awoke and saw the huge force, he cried out in fear, but Elisha remained calm. "Open his eyes, Lord," Elisha prayed, "that he might see." The Lord opened the eyes of the young man and he saw the Host of Heaven surrounding the Syrian Army. God had sent horses and chariots of fire to Elisha's defense.

God blinded the men of the army and Elisha led them to a city in Samaria. Elisha prayed once again and God opened their eyes. Those soldiers never attacked Israel again.

God doesn't leave people blind. He wants to open our physical eyes and spiritual eyes. It's a matter of finding out how to get our eyes open. We must want to be open and want to change. We can't be so content in life with our four walls that we don't want to make adjustments to the influence and direction of the Holy Spirit. There is more to seeing Jesus and serving Jesus than just going to church. We must be responsible and committed to Jesus and His teachings. We have a responsibility to be sure that the influences in our lives are godly ones. We don't have to listen to the devil or fall prey to his devices. In Jesus, we can be free and we can see clearly.

Chapter 9

Seeking to Be Our Best

Nine Men on the Field

I grew up playing baseball and like many young men dreamed of a major league career. One of the important lessons I learned from sports was, for a team to be a success, every member has to be functioning at his best. A baseball team has to have nine men out there on the field who are ready to play as if it were the most important game of the season. Every player must be alert and focused on the action of the moment.

A good team has members who can do their job. It needs good relief pitchers and pinch hitters just as it needs good starters. A team needs every one of them functioning and ready to play when called upon.

Every player must be focused on doing his job well. This brings success not only to the team, but to each individual player. We need that as Christians too. As a body of believers, we've been given a job to do in God's kingdom. We are to take the gospel to the world. As individuals we have our own day-by-day job of walking with Jesus. To do both of these things we must be alert and focused upon the Lord.

We want to function at our best at all times. This isn't as easy as it sounds. Many of us know what we're supposed to do for the Lord, but we're not doing it. Others of us do not know what we're supposed to be doing, but if we seek the Lord and seek to see Him clearly, He will show us.

What is the whole sum of the gospel? It is *reconciliation*. According to Paul in Second Corinthians 4, the purpose of Jesus' coming is to reconcile us to God and to show us how we can be a part of that plan. To be reconciled means to come back into a right relationship with God—a relationship of soundness, healing, wholeness, love, joy, and strength. That's what serving Jesus is about. It's an exciting and challenging way of life.

Unfortunately, today many of us are apathetic because we don't let God stir us. We don't do what

God says to get ourselves stirred up and so we're unconcerned, unfocused, and unproductive in His kingdom.

Jesus spoke about this in a message to the church at Ephesus in Revelation 2:4 when He said they had left their first love. Though they were still working for the Lord, they had lost their vision and were not working out of love but out of duty. He told the church at Laodicea that they were neither cold nor hot. They were only lukewarm (Revelation 3:16). These Christians had grown apathetic and needed to be stirred up once again.

The Christian life requires constant stirring so we can see clearly. We all grow weary at times and must seek rest. Jesus offers us rest. Rest and refreshing should be followed with a renewed zeal for the work. If it isn't, maybe we're not simply resting; maybe we've fallen asleep. We should heed the words of Paul and "awake to righteousness" (I Corinthians 15:34).

It's easier to relax and let life go on without us. When we're sick with the flu, we are prone to ignore things that used to please us. We can't get the energy to get up and get going, because we don't feel like it.

Just as the flu can steal our physical strength, apathy will steal our spiritual vision. It will keep us from being our very best for the Lord. We need to maintain our enthusiasm, so we can be productive and positive.

How can we keep ourselves stirred up, excited about God, focused upon Jesus, and enthusiastic about what we can do for Him? It comes through prayer—asking the Lord to change us so we can see Jesus more effectively. When we can see Jesus, then all of the rest of life will come into focus and we will be able to see how we're supposed to live.

Bob Welsh of the Oakland A's had to make a decision to renew his contract with the A's or become a free agent. He said, "Things came into focus and there was no doubt. I've followed my heart all my life." When everything focused for him, he had no doubts about what he wanted to do. We need that same kind of focus and certainty in following Jesus.

We want to be stirred up and excited about living for Jesus. We want to get off our pews and start functioning in the kingdom as God intended. It's a sad fact that in the Church many of us don't function; we merely exist. That's one of the problems we have in the Body of Christ. We are not nearly as effective as we could be in winning the world to Christ. If the Church can't see Jesus, how will the world?

When we get caught in problems, we often return to our old patterns of thought, and the old ways of doing things. We go around in circles. God wants to show us the way to get out of the circle of problems, doubts, discouragement and apathy. He will show us a new pattern and deliver us from our old ways.

There is a pattern for everything. There's a pattern for building cars and there is a pattern for sewing dresses. We have to learn new patterns to live the kind of life Jesus wanted for us. The Bible is a pattern for righteous living and it shows us how to live according to its pattern.

Here are a few of the patterns we find in the Bible:

The pattern for salvation is to believe in our heart and confess with our mouth that Jesus Christ is Lord (Romans 10:9-10).

The pattern for our thought life is to think on things that are pure, good, honest, just, and lovely (Philippians 4:8).

The pattern for living an abundant, overcoming life of love and service to others is the life of Jesus (II Corinthians 8:14). The more we see Him as the pattern the stronger, happier, healthier, more loving our life becomes. As a result, others will see Jesus because He will be patterned in us.

The Drifters

The best way to avoid wandering around in circles is to follow the path laid out by Jesus. We get in trouble when we drift away from truth and reality, from good counsel, guidance, peace, wisdom, and all the other things God shows us in His Word.

My ancestors, the Jews, drifted around the desert because they lost sight of their goal: the promised land. They drifted because they lost sight of a God who was big enough to take them into that land.

It seems like the hardest thing for people to do these days is to remain stable. As church members, we can look around and see people who drift into the church for a while, and then drift out again. They are not stable and their Christian lives reflect their instability. They are wandering Christians who never reach the promised land.

Recently, several men formed a movie production company. They were making low budget films of five million dollars or less (in these days that is a low budget film) and they were making money on their movies. Unfortunately, they drifted away from their original idea increasing their productions to 15 or 20 million dollars. Soon, they went bankrupt. They had the right vision but they didn't keep it. Losing that vision cost them hundreds of millions of dollars.

Whenever we lose sight of a goal, we risk never reaching it. Jesus is our goal, our example and if we lose sight of Jesus, we will lose sight of who we are as Christians. We will never know the fullness of life He wants us to enjoy.

My favorite singing group, The Moody Blues, sang, "Whenever I feel I'm losing my way, the power of your love remains." God's love is always there for us. It draws people back who have drifted away. James 4:8 tells us to "draw nigh to God, and he will draw nigh to you." If we find ourselves drifting away from the Lord and we draw back to Him, His love is there to receive us. Anytime we take a step toward the Lord, He will meet us on the road back home.

Not long ago, I felt impressed to track down some friends I haven't spoken to in years. They were divorced, but I managed to find one of the children and get the mother's phone number. I called her and we had a long talk about the past and then I said, "Let me pray for you." She said, "Please do."

This woman had been away from the Lord, but she was trying to draw closer to Him again. The Lord wanted to draw closer to her and I think that is why He impressed me to call her. She needed God's grace to come into her heart so she could see Jesus better.

Sometimes when people backslide, they don't see the way back because of the condemnation and guilt they feel. It can take them a long time to find their way back because they feel they let the Lord down, but God always wants to draw people back.

Wise Men Seek Him

Jesus said in Matthew 5:6, "Blessed are they which do hunger and thirst after righteousness: for they shall be filled." If we are not hungry, it's likely we won't sit down at the table for a meal. Often, we are not truly hungry for God. We won't sit down at His table and enjoy the bread of His Word.

We need to be like the Samaritan woman who Jesus met at a well. He told her He could give her living water so her thirst would be satisfied. This woman wanted the water Jesus offered. When she received it, it didn't come from the well. It flowed up from within her own spirit. When we hunger and thirst for God, we will be satisfied with living water and living bread. Jesus gave us access to these things when He offered Himself to the world.

When I visited Israel, I saw the little star in the church on Manger Square in Bethlehem, reported to be the birthplace of Jesus. The wise men who traveled so far to Bethlehem looking for a newborn king, followed a star. As scholars they knew that Moses foretold the coming of Jesus when he wrote, "There shall come a Star out of Jacob, and a Scepter shall rise out of Israel"(Numbers 24:17).

Those men were searchers in the Word. They knew the Scriptures and they searched the Scriptures, because they wanted to prove the words of Moses. In seeking Jesus, the King of the Jews, they confirmed the truth of the scriptures when they found Jesus. They had a hunger for God, were fed by His Word and God filled their hunger with His truth.

We have to ask God continually to lead us and give us the hunger for the truth in His Word. I think we all catch a glimpse of the Lord when we come to Him for salvation, but then, too often we camp for a while and lose our vision.

This happens in the natural too. People see all right one day and then suddenly their eyes start getting blurry for a variety of reasons. Maybe it's caused by pressure on a nerve, maybe it comes from worry and anxiety, maybe they were hit on the head, maybe their eyes are changing with age. Few people are fortunate enough to have 20/20 vision all their lives. If things start to get blurry, the wise individual goes to a doctor to find out what the problem is. None of us want to give up our eyesight.

I think most of those who attend church, have seen Jesus at one time, but then they lost the vision. We have grown comfortable sitting on a church pew and we fail to work at keeping our vision sharp and clear. We need the vision restored, so we can go on to an even greater and clearer vision.

Negatives and Positives

If there are positive things that help us see, there are also negative things that keep us from seeing. The negatives may often seem to be stronger than the positives. As difficult as it may be, we have to break out of the negatives and reestablish the positives.

The law of inertia says it is much easier to move an object in motion than to start moving an object that is at rest. The negative world is stronger when we rest in it and in bondage to it. When we have enough light to show us the way out and the strength to keep us out, our positive world becomes stronger than the negative.

What negatives stop people from seeing Jesus or even seeking Him? Apathy is one as we have already discussed. Another problem, closely related to apathy, is spiritual burnout. We strain our spiritual eyes looking in only one direction all the time and our vision becomes burned out.

Spiritual burnout describes the condition of being tired, unproductive, and struggling to keep our head above water. Often this problem arises, not because we have lagged behind, but because we have run ahead of the Lord. We can't see Jesus if we are way out in front of God's plan. In the natural, physical world, sound words of advice tell us that proper care of the body through diet, rest, and recreation will prevent physical burnout. We experience spiritual burnout because we don't follow the sound advice of God's Word. We carry the cares and the burdens of life on our shoulders instead of casting our cares upon the Lord (I Peter 5:7).

Jesus never intended for us to carry our burdens alone. He never intended for us to try to do everything for ourselves. He wants us to lean on Him, to rely upon Him. He doesn't want us to worry or to be afraid and He doesn't want us to get into strife or try to live our new life in the flesh. We do ourselves harm when we try to live our way instead of living God's way. That's when burnout can occur.

Most people struggling with either apathy or burnout don't want to see anything after a while. They are content just to be saved. They get settled in their apathy, their vision grows dim and their lives, as Christians, become boring and unfulfilling. Salvation is vitally important, but Jesus is so much more than our Savior. Salvation is only the beginning of God's many blessings.

Walk in the Light

I had read and heard there was a great spiritual darkness in western Europe and when I went there to minister, I found that with few exceptions it was true. Most of what the people say is negative, if they speak at all. Since the Christians in this region hardly speak the Word, they don't walk in the light of the Scriptures.

There was one woman I met in Europe who was having problems with the negatives that come against us all. She was getting confused in her mind and was discouraged and depressed. She was eating too much and putting on weight and feeling bad about herself, which only caused her to eat even more.

I told her, "This is an attack of Satan against your mind. He wants to keep you in darkness. You have to rebuke the devil." But, she wouldn't rebuke the devil because she didn't believe she had authority to do so. She didn't know that the Bible said "resist the devil and he will flee from you" (James 4:7).

God gave her a dream that the devil was after her husband. She rebuked the devil in her dream and the devil left. She could rebuke the devil in her dreams when he threatened someone she loved, but she would not stand up for herself. So her problems increased and so did her weight. She grew more and more frustrated because she didn't walk in the light of what I told her and what her dream was trying to tell her. Finally, after I had counseled her several times, she began to understand. She realized God had given her the authority to stand up to the devil. When she began to do it, the darkness began to lift. Eventually, she could see more clearly and she is doing much better today.

We have to walk in the light of what we know from the Word of God on a consistent, day-by-day basis. When the oil light on the car dash lights up, we can either heed that light and take care of the car immediately or replace an engine later.

The Word of God is filled with direction for our lives, but we must walk in its light and heed its warnings. If we don't, we will suffer the consequences. The Bible might be seen as our Manufacturer's Guidelines. God, our designer and creator, has given us all the information we need to live well. If we ignore those guidelines, we will not see clearly, we will not be able to follow in Jesus' footsteps and we will not be able to see the path the Word illuminates.

If we are smart, we will trust a good mechanic to repair our car. He will have the proper equipment and the knowledge to use the equipment. We expect the job to be done right because the mechanic is the expert in this case. We put our car in his hands and trust him to find the problem and fix it.

When we have problems with our spiritual engine, God is able to identify the problem and help us correct it quickly. He wants our spiritual vision functioning properly all the time.

Chapter 10

Overcoming Fear

Focus or Fear

I heard a story about a statue of Christ in a certain country. Many people would make pilgrimages to this statue year after year to show their devotion. When they left, it was customary for them to bid the statue goodbye. It was as though they were leaving Christ behind. These pilgrims had no concept of taking the Lord with them. They didn't know He could be with them all the time. Their view of Jesus was limited and as a result they did not know Him or His power in their everyday lives. Theirs was a religion of fear rather than faith.

In the Body of Christ today, we must see Jesus as the Lord of our lives. We need to see Him as someone who will always be there for us. Jesus promised in Hebrews 13:5, "I will never leave thee, nor forsake thee."

Sometimes it's hard for us to see that. We say, "I don't feel like Jesus is with me right now." We don't go by feelings, we receive it by faith. Faith is not based on feelings. If we believe what He says, then we will see what He says. Without faith our vision and understanding of Jesus is limited, too narrow, or wrong.

Fear is another problem that will keep us from seeing Jesus. We saw fear at work when we studied about the blind man Jesus healed. The blind man's parents were "blinded" by their fear of the religious leaders so they could not see Jesus. They refused to acknowledge the power of Jesus to heal because they didn't want to be put out of the synagogue.

Fear doesn't come from God. It comes from the devil. The Bible says, "God has not given us the spirit of fear: but of power, and of love, and of a sound mind" (II Timothy 1:7). Fear can work in any area and can come at any time, so we have to be vigilant and rebuke it in the name of Jesus.

We cannot let fear get a foothold in our lives. Fear can easily snowball into something so big we become controlled by the fear rather than by faith. Fear can cloud our judgment and wreck our thinking. It can keep us from seeing Jesus as He is. No problem, no amount of fear is bigger than Jesus. We must not let fear tell us any different.

Jesus was in a boat one day, crossing the Sea of Galilee with His disciples. A sudden storm came up and the disciples thought the boat was going to sink. They were afraid of drowning, but Jesus, free from fear, was sleeping peacefully in the boat. The disciples thought He wasn't concerned about them or their safety. They woke Him up and questioned His lack of care over their safety. They saw their fear of the storms and the waves more clearly than they saw Jesus.

After Jesus rebuked the wind and the sea and everything was still, He turned to the disciples and asked, "Why are ye so fearful? how is it that ye have no faith?" (Mark 4:40).

Like the disciples in the boat, the storms that buffet us can look very frightening and we often doubt that Jesus cares about us. If we allow our faith to disappear, our fear will grow as our vision of Jesus grows dim. If we deal with our fear, our faith will return and our vision of Jesus will clear. We must keep a "faith maintenance" system working in our lives and it has to be done every day. The devil, through our mind, tries to bring fear every day to cause us to mistrust God and to doubt His concern. To counteract fear, we must keep our faith strong through prayer, praise, and reading the Word of God.

Being able to see clearly isn't important only in a spiritual sense. Seeing clearly in the spirit is the first step toward seeing clearly in other ways. Our objective is seeing clearer and clearer all the time in every area of our lives—the right spiritual decisions, the right business decisions, where to go, what to do, where to move, choosing the right job, the right friends, and the right investments.

Someone has said, "When you don't know in which direction to turn, then turn to Jesus." That is very good advice. We can't truly find our way through life until we have found our way to Jesus. We cannot truly see how to live until we have caught a true vision of Jesus and that vision must not be clouded with fear.

Keep the Light

When I receive a revelation from God's Word, I put that revelation in my heart. Even though doubts try to cloud the vision, I believe the love, peace, wisdom, and joy is still there, because of what I read in God's Word. I've seen it through the eyes of faith in my spirit. We all can see Jesus. We all can see what the Word has to tell us about the Lord. No matter what comes against us, the truth is still there. Jesus doesn't change even if the circumstances around us have.

If we get revelation one day, we must not doubt it the next day. We can't doubt in the dark what

God has shown us in the light. When it's nice and clear, we can see. When confusion, doubt or fear come, we may not be able to see as clearly. Though we can't see as clearly, we don't have to doubt. When we receive revelation about a truth for our lives, quickly the trials and tribulations may come.

There is no reason to let fear control us because of what is happening in the world today. Jesus predicted all these things would come to pass. He said, "These things I have spoken unto you, that in Me ye might have peace. In the world ye shall have tribulation: but be of good cheer; I have overcome the world" (John 16:33). Our rest and our peace is in Jesus. No matter what we hear going on in the world, we shouldn't let it steal our peace and our love and bring fear and worry. We keep looking unto Jesus. We turn our eyes upon the Lord.

We have to walk in the light we have now and what we know to be true now and then we will receive more light and knowledge. First John 1:7 says, "But if we walk in the light, as He is in the light, we have fellowship one with another, and the blood of Jesus Christ His Son cleanseth us from all sin."

We must see Jesus as our Savior, deliverer, healer, counselor, and guide. Seeing Him as our counselor is difficult for many people. It is hard for them to receive and obey the counsel of the Lord because so often it seems to go against the flesh or human logic. No matter what we feel or what we think, we have to walk in the light of what we see in Jesus and His Word.

Walking in the light is the key to avoiding what happened to the disciples. We must focus on the situation from God's perspective. Sure, things may look dark and scary from our point of view. It certainly did to the disciples when they all ran from the garden at the time of Jesus' arrest. But, Jesus was in control of that situation and if we will let Him, He will be in control of any situation we may face today. We don't have to fear if we walk in the light of what Jesus has said in His Word. Through Him we can receive the solution to our fear.

In a good movie, with a good director, the camera beautifully catches every detail of the scene. The director's eye is everywhere and he tells the story of the movie, as he sees it, through the eye of the camera.

A good painter will see the detail of the scene he's painting. He creates the whole atmosphere by painting what he sees. Someone else can paint the same scene and miss all the details because they don't see what the painter sees. Good artists catch things other people don't see. We would say the painter has a good eye.

When it comes to spiritual matters, we have to have a good eye all the time. We must keep focused on Jesus and look at things from His perspective. His is the only true perspective because He sees everything.

You've probably heard people say they were worrying about so many things—a fight with their spouse or problems on the job—and as they were driving along, not thinking about what they were doing, something happened. They had a wreck because they didn't see clearly. They were seeing their problem in their mind instead of thinking about what they were doing.

That's what happens to us spiritually. We let the circumstances surrounding us make us fearful or worried. Then we forget the promises Jesus made to us. We stop seeing Him as the answer to our every need. We try to figure things out for ourselves instead of seeing Jesus. Certainly it's better to see than to stumble around in the darkness of doubt and fear and unbelief.

Many of us don't realize our lives are based on what we believe—either in the negative or the positive. Everything we do rises out of what we believe inside. One person might say, "I can't get on that plane. I know it's going to crash." Someone else would say, "Oh, we're going to have a wonderful plane ride. The view from there is fantastic." It all depends upon what we believe and the point of view we hold.

Who Am I?

The most important point of view is how we see Jesus. Is He the Christ, the Son of the living God to us? Is He the one who never leaves us or forsakes us? How we see Jesus will determine how we handle the ups and downs of life. If we are trusting in a loving Savior, we will not let fear steal our vision of Him.

As Jesus became more and more popular with the people, the Pharisees became more and more concerned about His popularity. The miracles of healing, deliverance and compassion that He demonstrated through the power of God in His ministry were causing the people to spread the word about God's love and provision for the people. The Pharisees sent spies out who, when they returned, reported that they were amazed that He answered their questions with such authority.

It was at this point that Jesus turned to His disciples and said, "Whom do men say that I the Son of man am?" (Matthew 16:13). In other words, He was saying, "The people have seen Me and what I've done, but who do they say I am? What have they learned? What has touched their hearts?"

With such power in His ministry and such authority in His words, the disciples said that the people thought Jesus might be John the Baptist returned from the grave. Or they thought He might be Elijah or Jeremiah or one of the prophets. Obviously the people didn't see Jesus clearly and they were trying to make Him into someone else. They were trying to compare Him to someone they already knew. Even though Jesus was a prophet, He was also much more than a prophet and this is what the people needed to see, but they didn't have an accurate view of Jesus.

We don't always think carefully about what we believe. We never question what we're thinking or what we've heard or what we thought someone said. That is how satan can bring in confusion and fear. It's the devil's business to try to blind us with confusion, negative influences, fear, doubt, and unbelief. He works overtime and we have to battle what satan brings against us in order to break through, to get the light, and to see what we need to see.

The people who saw Jesus as just a prophet had not truly turned their eyes upon Him. They could not see through the veil of their fears or religious beliefs or hardness of heart. Those who followed Jesus saw Him much more clearly.

Jesus then asked the disciples the most important question in life, "But whom say ye that I am? And Simon Peter answered and said, Thou art the

Christ, the Son of the living God. And Jesus answered and said unto him, Blessed art thou, Simon Bar-jona: for flesh and blood hath not revealed it unto thee, but My Father which is in heaven" (Matthew 16:15-17).

What Jesus meant was, "Peter, no human being could have told you who I am. These people don't know who I am. My Father in heaven is showing you who I am." Heaven shows us who and what Jesus is by the Holy Spirit, the Spirit of truth. Jesus offered Peter the "keys to the kingdom" and, with these same keys, we have access to all God promised us through Jesus. The Lord came to bring life, hope, peace, righteousness, joy, and so much more. The keys give us power and authority in God and, through His Word, we can see and believe that we have these promises through Christ Jesus.

Unfortunately, we can see clearly one day and the next day everything is blurry once again. Peter saw Jesus as the Christ, the Messiah, the anointed Son of God. At that moment of revelation it was as though a light had come inside Peter and he knew beyond a shadow of a doubt that Jesus was God. Later, as often happens with so many of us, Peter had a problem and he let something blur his vision. Although he had the keys to the kingdom, Peter challenged the direction Jesus had chosen and it brought him a sharp rebuke from the Lord.

Peter had caught a clear glimpse of Jesus, but he let it slip away. He couldn't see that Jesus had come to this world to die for all mankind and through His resurrection to offer all of mankind the gift of abundant and eternal life. Jesus' words were frightening to Peter and to the other disciples as well. None of them wanted to hear what Jesus had to say about His death. They had their eyes set on a glorious earthly kingdom. They failed to understand the scope of the kingdom Jesus offered, an eternal kingdom that He wanted to establish within their hearts. In Peter's case, he focused on fear instead of the promise offered and, for Peter, fear snuffed out the light.

Someone or something is always out there to take our light—the world, the devil, the flesh, discouragement, fear, and many other things. We have to guard ourselves against these things every day. We have to keep our eyes on Jesus and keep our faith strong in Him.

If someone showed us how to make 20 million dollars every year, would we ignore that knowledge? Would we misplace it or forget it? I doubt it! Yet the knowledge of Jesus is far more valuable than 20 million dollars. Just as we would hold on to the knowledge that will bring earthly riches, we must hold on to the knowledge Jesus gives us to achieve eternal riches through Him.

At one time, Simon Peter saw the light. He received a revelation that Jesus was the Christ. Later, he denied Jesus. He ran away. Unfortunately, for Peter, this is the one event we remember most when we think about poor Peter. Perhaps there is another reason we remember Peter in this way. I think we recall this weakness in Peter, because we have all been guilty of the same thing.

We receive the light in our heart and mind, but then something happens and we deny the truth we heard. The natural mind tries to convince us not to believe. Fear, pain, trials and tribulations come in to take the light. We listen to the negative words and unbelief of other people. We have to hold on to each ray of light God shows us in the Word and let nothing and no one take it from us.

Jesus had given the disciples light on what was to take place in the future. He told the disciples many times He would go to Jerusalem and die and then rise again. They heard, but they really didn't hear. Perhaps they didn't want to hear because it was too horrible for them to think about. In any case, the word Jesus gave them was replaced by wrong thinking that resulted in poor vision.

Jesus' ministry following His resurrection was devoted to rebuilding their faith and enlarging their understanding of who He is. He reminded them of who they were and what they believed concerning Him. We must take the time to do that also. We must have it established in our mind that Jesus is the Son of God—our Savior and our Lord.

In His appearance to Peter on the shores of the Sea of Tiberias, Jesus gave him a mission to fulfill (John 21). From this point, Peter saw his life in Christ clearly. He did not waiver in the mission that lay ahead of him. Just as Peter regained his faith and his sight, when we keep looking at Jesus, we will find the spiritual and physical strength to fulfill our mission in life.

When we learn to give Him the honor and the glory and we ask Him to open our eyes, He'll do it. We may be less than perfect and we may make mistakes, just as Peter did. All we are asked to do is to walk in the light we have and increase that light by reading the Word and following God's plan.

Jesus will open our eyes. Then we use our authority—the keys to the kingdom which God has given us—against anything that tries to bring blurry vision to us—fears, confusion, people, bad doctrine, and hardness of heart.

Chapter 11

Seeing God's Point of View

Whose Point of View?

We all have our own point of view about everything in life. Ten people can look at the same object and there will be ten different points of view. Listen to ten eyewitnesses to a traffic accident and every one of them will have a different story to tell. Who is right? Possibly all of them, because each is telling the story from his or her point of view.

Take a group of people to a concert and some of them will say it was great, and others will say, "Well, it wasn't that good." They came to the concert with certain standards in their mind and they judged the concert by those standards.

Everyone has a point of view. How do you see this person? How do you perceive that situation? How do you judge this action? There are many points of view, each unique to any one individual. This isn't necessarily bad if we can keep in mind that ours is only one point of view and someone else's view might be as valid as ours. When we refuse to consider any other point of view but our own, we can get into trouble. If we look at life and God in only one way, we might not be seeing clearly.

So many of us believe the wrong things in life and we blame God for the results of our wrong beliefs and wrong thoughts. It's not God's fault. We make our trouble most of the time, but it's easier to blame someone else than to acknowledge responsibility for our actions. Wrong thinking is one more problem that can stop us from seeing Jesus clearly.

People see things in certain ways because of their preconceived ideas. All sorts of people and events influence our point of view. We learn from our parents, friends, past experiences, teachers and the media, to mention just a few of the many forces which influence our thinking and our choices. Much of what we experience is colored by what we know from the past. That means we may not always see things exactly as they are.

Let's suppose I'm the general manager of a baseball team sitting down with one of my players. "The fans like you," I might say. "But, behind the scenes, your teammates don't like you because you're causing problems all the time. The fans think you're great. You hit a home run and they want you to come out and bow. But, behind the scenes you're nothing but trouble. Your actions don't line up with your image."

One well-known athlete made a commercial saying, "Image is everything." This is usually true in the world of sports and entertainment, but image is also deceiving at times. How do we see things? How do we see people? Is the image the real thing? How do we see Jesus? Do we see Him as He is or do we see Him by a preconceived point of view?

Do Baptists see Jesus one way and Catholics another way and Charismatics still another way? Why? Aren't we all serving the same Jesus? Obviously, the answer is yes.

Fortunately, Jesus comes to each of us on an individual basis. He meets us where we are in spite of all our preconceived ideas and prejudices and misunderstandings. He came to me when I wasn't certain He was real. I wasn't sure I believed He was the Son of God. Still, He came to me and revealed Himself to me.

Jesus is always true to Himself. He will come to us where we are, but He will not change into something else to suit us. We must change to suit Him and, if our preconceived ideas are wrong, we must change them to see Jesus clearly.

In the church, we often see Jesus one way and that view may influence our perspective of Him throughout our lives. Many people learn from their church experience that Jesus is hard or demanding. Or, perhaps they grew up seeing their parents treating one another hard and this treatment was born out as they observed other families in their church. So, they think that's the way they're supposed to treat people. Naturally, their view of God is going to reflect what they have seen and learned in church and through their parents.

Often, we need to have our thoughts and beliefs challenged. If our beliefs are sound, they will stand up to the challenge. Jesus challenges our faith and what we believe by pointing us back to the Word of God. The devil challenges what we believe by trying to plant doubts and fears in our mind. We challenge ourselves in what we believe by how we react to these other challenges.

Everything comes down to our point of view, but many times we don't realize that our strong beliefs are nothing more than our point of view. And it may not be the right point of view. If it doesn't line up with what God says in His Word then something needs to be changed. When we cannot confirm our beliefs through God's Word, we should be willing to change our beliefs and make them line up with what God is saying.

Have you ever had someone say to you, "I see, from my point of view, that if you will do this, things will be better?" Sometimes they are right and you would be wise to follow their advice, but at other times you realize their point of view isn't an accurate one and you'd be better off not listening to them.

On the other hand, have you ever thought if people would see things from your point of view everything would be so much better? That may be true some of the time, but I doubt it is true all the time.

All of us must be willing to change the way we look at things. It's all a matter of the point of view we choose. God sees everything from His point of view and since He knows everything, His point of view will certainly be the only accurate one. He wants things done from His point of view. His way is the best way—always.

The Lord says, "My thoughts are not your thoughts, neither are your ways my ways...For as the heavens are higher than the earth, so are my ways higher than your ways, and my thoughts than your thoughts" (Isaiah 55:8,9). If you have ever stood at the highest window of a tall building and looked out over a city, you will get the idea of this Scripture. God looks down from His heavenly vantage point and sees it all. More than that, He sees inside the human heart. Hebrews 4:12 says His word is a "discerner of the thoughts and intents of the heart." God sees what is going on outside us and inside us as well.

We can trust His point of view and should be eager to make our view the same as His. The best part of all is that God's view of us is through eyes of love. Even though He is aware of all our weaknesses, He still looks at us in love. If we have received His Son, then we have received His righteousness and that is how He sees us. It should be how we see ourselves.

Isn't it sad that we won't give God the same benefit He gives us? So often we don't view God in the right way. We don't see Jesus as He truly is. Why are we so quick to believe the devil's lies that God doesn't care about us? The devil tells us God doesn't know what we are going through, or he tells us God is punishing us with a trial or sickness. When we believe those things we're looking at God from the wrong point of view.

Life can be compared to a courtroom trial. Both the defense attorney and the prosecuting attorney are going to try to get the jury to see his point of view. There are two points of view we must choose between—what God says in His Word and what the devil whispers in our ear. The deciding vote in this matter is ours. We will believe what we choose to believe and, in the end, we will see what we believe.

What stops us from seeing in the right way? I believe one of the obstacles to good vision is *stubbornness*. We are *stubborn* about seeing a point of view different from the one we've always held or always heard from others. This can mean we are not letting good things into our lives, because we refuse to see things clearly. In spiritual sight, accepting the gift of good vision without prejudice is a prerequisite to seeing clearly. We must be willing to put aside our preconceived ideas and accept the Lord in faith.

If we were to go to a remote area of South America or Africa where the gospel has not been preached, we might find people who would accept the gospel story very easily and eagerly. They have no prejudices, no doctrine, no cynicism, and no preconceived ideas to keep them from seeing and accepting the truth of God's Word.

We would begin our outreach by preaching about Jesus as Savior. We would tell the story of His life and His love and read scriptures to them explaining the salvation message. With open minds they would see Jesus as their Savior and accept His gift of salvation like children opening presents on Christmas morning.

The next night we will preach Jesus is the healer. We will read story after story from the Bible about the people Jesus healed and explain that He took the stripes upon His back so they could be healed also. They will begin to see and accept Him as their healer and they will be healed. Miracles of healing will take place among them because they see Jesus as He is.

On the third night, we will preach Jesus as the Prince of Peace and give many scriptures to support this picture. The people are going to see Him as peace and receive peace in their heart, mind, emotions, and body.

Then, we will teach Jesus as joy and we will have all these people laughing in the joy of the Lord. They will see Jesus as the Bible portrays Him because they have no reason to see Him otherwise.

Jesus talked about having the faith of a little child. He said this was how we enter into the kingdom of heaven (Luke 18:17). Simple, childlike faith has no preconditions and no prejudices. Perhaps this is why children seem to see Jesus better than adults. They come to Him believing what He says. They very often receive miracles in answer to their faith. Their vision is focused upon the Lord.

I Thought It Would Happen Like This

In Second Kings 5, we read the story of a man who sought his healing. He almost missed receiving it because of his preconceived ideas and his failure to keep his vision focused upon his goal.

The man's name was Naaman. He was the commander of the Syrian Army and he was suffering from leprosy. Naaman heard from an Israelite maid about the prophet Elisha who was able to heal. He saw himself being healed because he believed that report.

So he asked the King of Syria for a letter to the King of Israel outlining his need. When he arrived in Jerusalem he presented the king with his request for healing. The king tore his garments in despair, because he knew he could not heal this important Syrian officer.

Fortunately, Elisha heard about the king's visitor and sent word to the king to send Naaman to him. The Syrian general with his horses and chariot and his entourage of soldiers and servants came to the prophet's house. Elisha did not come out of his house to greet the general with great ceremony. Instead, he sent his servant out with instructions for Naaman to go and wash in the Jordan River seven times (II Kings 5:9-10).

Naaman had a preconceived idea about how he would be healed and he refused to listen to the servant's message. He left Elisha's house angry. Naaman lost sight of his goal—to be healed.

Many of us have our own preconceived ideas about how something is going to happen. We want our healing to come just as it did for our grandmother who had so much faith. We want to dictate our terms to God and have Him act according to our expectations. But, it doesn't happen like that.

We don't know how God is going to move in our lives unless He chooses to tell us personally. He may give us something specific to do and it may be as bizarre as the instructions Elisha gave to Naaman. What He tells us may go against our own ideas. What will we do then? Will we obey and receive our answer to prayer or will we go away angry and upset because it didn't happen the way we thought it should?

There is a sure way to know what God wants us to do. His Word gives us many guidelines for living. When we have found the truth from God's Word, we must stand upon it and never let anything get in the way of our vision. We must know with certainty what God has said to us. We have to know beyond a doubt that it is from the Lord.

We can't mistake preconceived ideas, things we've heard from others or rigid church doctrine for God's Word and God's direction. Many of us have preconceived ideas about God and the way He answers prayer. Often we find out those ideas are wrong.

Naaman lost the vision he once had for his healing and he went away from Elisha's house in anger. He lost his faith, his confidence, and he almost lost his healing. Only when he realized that his healing was more important than his preconceived ideas did he stop to listen to one of his servants.

His servant said, "If the prophet had bid thee do some great thing, wouldest thou not have done it? how much rather then, when he saith to thee, Wash, and be clean?" (II Kings 5:13). In other words he was saying, "Hey, it's an easy thing he's telling you to do. Why not give it a try?"

Naaman had come expecting a big, impressive ceremony. Instead, he had been asked to do something simple, even humbling. His mind, which was set in one direction and fueled by his anger, made him lose his focus and forget why he had come to Israel. When his servant spoke to him, he realized his need was more important than his pride. He listened to the counsel, did what Elisha had instructed him to do and he received his healing.

New Vision

As I was driving around Tulsa one day, the name of an optical clinic caught my eye. It was called the

New Vision Eye Clinic. People go there to get their eyes tested and, if necessary, they are fitted with glasses or contacts. In a spiritual sense, that's what we all need. We need new vision, vision that needs correction from time to time.

I have a friend who wears glasses and he recently had the prescription changed. His old glasses were scratched and his eyes had changed, so he wasn't seeing as well as he should. The new glasses began to give him problems too, because a defect was causing a reflection. He had to take the glasses back for an adjustment so he could see clearly.

Each of us has to adjust our spiritual vision thousands and thousands of times throughout our lives. It's thousands of adjustments in different areas; with God, with our relationships, friends, job, work and in every facet of life.

I met an elderly gentleman the other day and we were talking about relationships in general and marriage in particular. He confided in me, "I've been married more than 38 years, but there is no fulfillment for me. We didn't see what we were getting into when we rushed into marriage." This man is not alone. Many people don't take the time to see what is going on within a relationship. We have to know what adjustments need to be made and we need to keep a new, fresh, focused vision all the time. This will help us avoid making mistakes that would be regretted later on.

When we take pictures with a camera that has a manual focus, we must adjust the camera lens every time we move to a new position. We may take several pictures of the same subject, but from different angles and distances. Each picture needs the proper focus. Otherwise our photographs will come out blurry and distorted.

Life is like that too. We are always moving, always changing. We have to adjust the focus of our vision so it is always sharp and clear as we grow in life and as we take on new responsibilities. Over time, as the direction of our lives changes, adjustments have to be made to accommodate these changes. Otherwise, the vision we have of ourselves or of the Lord will be in danger of becoming blurred or distorted.

Have you ever been around a new Christian or do you remember when you first accepted the Lord as your Savior? The enthusiasm and love, felt by new Christians, is contagious. As a new-born Christian, we saw Jesus through eyes of wonder, faith, and love. Everything became brand new.

With time the newness seems to fade. Actually, we are experiencing change in vision, sometimes for the worse, but, hopefully, it changes for the better. We all grow in the Word or, at least, we should.

We no longer "as newborn babes, desire the sincere milk of the word" (I Peter 2:2), but rather desire "strong meat [which] belongeth to them that are of full age" (Hebrews 5:14). Our level of maturity changes and our vision should change with it.

Doctors tell us the eyes of newborn babies don't focus well, but as the child grows, vision becomes stronger and clearer. We want that to be true of us in the spiritual realm as well. While we don't ever want to lose our first love for Jesus, we want our vision to grow stronger and clearer as we learn more about Him.

But, as I have said throughout this book, there are many things that try to hinder our vision. Often when we hear something from the Word of God that is new and exciting to us, our vision of Jesus is expanded and our faith grows. Then something comes along to discourage or disillusion us and the vision gets lost. We lose sight of what God has said in His Word. Like Naaman, we may even go away angry, never receiving what we were seeking from the Lord and, then, we fail to reach our goal.

In playing sports, shooting pictures or writing a book, one of the key points is to keep focused on the goal. Remember the kaleidoscopes we played with as children? We turned it to focus the pieces and see the different colors in the whole picture.

To see the beauty of Jesus, we must also keep in focus. That's one of the hardest things to do—to keep focused all the time. We must renew our vision each day if we are to remain focused on Jesus.

God's Point of View

One of my favorite westerns is *High Noon* starring Gary Cooper and Grace Kelly. When the movie was first made, everyone thought it was a bomb. It didn't click. Then, the film editor got the idea of showing a clock at different intervals to show time moving slowly toward noon. At 12 o'clock the train was coming to town with the bad guys, who had threatened to kill the character played by Gary Cooper. The townspeople and his wife wanted him to get out of town before the outlaws could carry out their plan.

The addition of the clock, bolstered by dramatic music, added to the suspense. These new elements, from the point of view of the film editor and the music director, changed the impact the movie had on the audience. The tick of the clock had a tremendous affect and *High Noon* became one of the greatest westerns ever made as well as an academy-award-winning movie.

Everything comes down to a point of view. During Desert Storm, the world watched closely what happened in Saudi Arabia and the Persian Gulf.

Each night on the evening news, we saw reports from that area of the world. There were many different reporters covering the various situations developing in the Middle East. All of them reported from different points of view and produced different reports on the same subject.

We see this same idea in the way the writers of the gospels told the story of Jesus' life. Some of the stories are the same in all four books, but they are told from different points of view. One writer may give more detail than the others to provide us with more light and more revelation.

Some people haven't figured that out yet. They say, "The Bible contradicts itself." No, it doesn't contradict itself. It simply offers a bigger picture of God's truth through the writing of many different individuals. We need to see the Bible in the right way—from God's point of view.

God wants our lives to reflect His point of view in each and every situation. He can take a life lacking interest and drama and turn it into something wonderful and good. Our part is to allow Him to put in the changes He desires. We must be willing to listen to His voice, no matter how still and small it might be in the midst of the clamor of the world.

God's Spirit Enables His Point of View

When I returned from Austria, I brought home a nice suit a new friend had given me. It was too small for me so I took the suit to a seamstress to have it altered. I always take something that needs to be altered to her because she does very good work. This time the seamstress looked the suit over and told me she didn't think she would be able to alter it.

I was disappointed because I assumed if she couldn't do it, then it was not likely anyone could. I was about to walk out of the shop when I felt prompted to ask, "Do you know anyone else who could do it?"

The woman said, "Yes," and she told me of a tailor in a shopping center in Tulsa. When I took the suit to him, he took a little knife out and cut into a seam to see if there was sufficient material for the alterations. He said he could do it and now I have a very nice, well-fitting suit to wear.

I believe it was the quiet voice of the Holy Spirit prompting me to ask if someone else could alter the suit. Some may think my suit problem too trivial a matter to concern God, but I don't. I have found God has answers for everything. If I will listen to Him and follow His direction, I can find those answers. From God's point of view, there are no problems, only solutions. That's why we need to see from God's point of view.

The Holy Spirit is here to water the Word in us so it can grow like a seed. He is here to help us see

God's point of view. The Holy Spirit sees everything. In my meetings I give words of knowledge for healing. I don't know the people, but the Holy Spirit knows them and He directs me so they can be healed.

I give the word and they come forward and get healed. That word is from the Holy Spirit's point of view and if they respond they receive a miracle.

Of course, there are always those who will not respond...and they don't receive. If we hold on to lies or doubts or fears in different areas, then we don't receive and we risk becoming angry and bitter. If we hold on to negative things our whole life, we never open ourselves up to another influence or point of view. We won't be able to trust anyone, not even God. We will struggle with problems all through life.

If we hold on to things contrary to God, this will distort our vision of God. If we are not changing with the times and growing in the Lord and are not trying to see clearly, our whole life could become bitter and futile.

We should be progressive in different areas and avenues and attitudes for freedom, ministry, health, and for life. We should not stay the same way day after day, month after month, year after year.

It's wrong attitudes that destroy people. We should ask ourselves, "Does God want me to have these bad attitudes?" Of course, the answer is no, God doesn't want us to have the bad attitudes that damage our lives. If bad attitudes consume us, not only will we be miserable, but we'll make life miserable for those around us as well.

It's time we change our attitudes and opinions. Many of us need to ease up, because we are so heavy and serious all the time. I've known people who take life so seriously they think the whole world hangs on the thread of what they do. They always seem to be intense. If we are supposed to be intense all the time, why would God tell us to have peace, joy, and light?

Jesus said, "Take My yoke upon you, and learn of Me; for I am meek and lowly in heart: and ye shall find rest unto your souls. For My yoke is easy, and My burden is light" (Matthew 11:29-30). God doesn't want us to be heavy; He wants us to be light.

The vision of such people is distorted because of worries and anxieties in their mind. They get spaced out, frantic, and frazzled. We keep in focus by seeing Jesus as our redeemer, our healer, and our friend. When that vision inside our spirit and mind gets stronger and stronger, then we will have more confidence in God and ourselves. As we dwell in the good, the bad will not distort our vision and our attitude will adjust to God's point of view.

We must see Jesus as what He says He is. It's a matter of believing it, receiving it, and letting the vision grow inside us with the truth becoming clearer and clearer.

We don't believe the truth of God and His Word because of wrong thinking and preconceived ideas. We have to see it from God's point of view because if we don't we're not going to see at all. The more our vision lines up with God's vision, the more clearly we will see and a greater clarity of thinking will come.

For instance, let's say we need healing. We're studying healing in the Word and praying earnestly for it, yet we don't see the healing take place. We are struggling to believe and keep our faith strong and our vision focused.

Then the thought comes, "You're not going to get healed because of what you did ten years ago. You're not going to get healed because you're not worthy." That is a condemning thought. It doesn't line up with the Word of God. Nowhere does the Bible say we have to earn healing or be worthy enough to receive it.

If we receive the condemning thought, we push away the light of healing. If, as a result of our faulty vision, the healing doesn't come as quickly as we thought or in the way we thought, we may give up. Many of us struggle with this every day.

If we are going to see Jesus clearly we must believe, receive, study and ask God to open our eyes. God's desire is for us to see clearly, free from distortion. We must continue to pray,

> "Lord, God help me see. Show me the truth from Your point of view. Give me wisdom, give me revelation, give me new teaching, give me a new hunger. Open my eyes, Lord. I want to see Jesus. In Jesus name, amen."

Chapter 12

Seeing Jesus in Ourselves

Who Is My Family?

One way we see Jesus is seeing Him in ourselves...and in each other. Seeing Jesus in one another is a part of the family relationship we enjoy as Christians. Have you ever noticed you can often identify people as Christians because Jesus shines forth in their lives? You can see the "family resemblance." It may be noticeable in a firm, confident handshake or a joyful smile or a peaceful look in their eyes. Something about them says they are part of the family.

But, who is Jesus' family? That question Jesus Himself asked in Mark 3:31-35. Jesus was surrounded by a crowd of followers, who were listening to Him teach, when something unusual happened. His family came and stood outside the place where He was teaching and called out to Him. The gospel tells us that the multitude sitting around Him said, "Behold, thy mother and thy brethren without seek for thee" (Mark 3:32).

There were so many people around Jesus, His mother and His brothers couldn't get to Him. Notice, Jesus did not say, "Make a way so My mother can come to Me." Instead Jesus startled everyone by saying, "Who is My mother, or My brethren?" After asking the question, He gave them the answer, "And He looked round about on them which sat about Him, and said, Behold My mother and My brethren! For whosoever shall do the will of God, the same is My brother, and My sister, and mother" (Mark 3:33-35).

In this passage Jesus shows us not only who *His* family is, but He also helps us see clearly who *our* family is. If we look at His words closely, we'll see that not all who say they are Christians are really a part of the family. That is because so many Christians are not doing the will of God. According to Jesus, "Whosoever shall do the will of God, *(or the Word which is God's will)* the same is My brother, and My sister, and mother." So not all Christians are His family.

Today, it seems real family is one of the hardest things to find. We have become a mobile society, moving easily and often from place to place. Even within the Body of Christ, we can feel isolated. It's hard to find good friends and true family when we come to a new place. Jesus tells us to look for those who are doing His will. When you find these people, you will have found His family.

Only those of like-minded faith and conviction and action are going to understand us. These are truly the members of our family and, as family members, we will grow together. We will be quick to respond to the needs of the family. If we believe in the full gospel and someone else does not, we may have difficulty fellowshiping with one another. I'm not teaching denominational isolation. I think everyone who is a Christian should love everyone else who is a Christian, but there are many people in the church who aren't Christians. They may be more of a hindrance than a help to our walk with the Lord. We should look for the "family resemblance" in those with whom we fellowship. Our true family is those who keep God's Word.

We like to think of Jesus bringing people together in love, peace, and harmony. Often He does, but Jesus also differentiates between people. He always makes a division between good and evil, right and wrong, those who belong to Him and those who don't. Those who belong to Him are those who obey Him. If we see someone keeping Jesus' Word, then we will see Jesus in that person.

Many people think wearing the label "Christian" is enough to make them family. They say, "Well, I'm under grace so I don't have to keep any commandments. I'm not under the law." That can sound nice, even scriptural, but it's just an excuse not to do something they don't want to do.

Jesus said, "A new commandment I give unto you, That ye love one another; as I have loved you, that ye also love one another. By this shall all men know that ye are My disciples, If ye have love one to another" (John 13:34-35). Everywhere I minister I ask, "Is everyone in the Body of Christ walking in love?" The answer I inevitably receive is, "No." Yet, it's a commandment! Why aren't some doing it? Because there are some who don't want to obey Jesus. We can't see Jesus in people who refuse to love others.

If we willfully disobey a law, we are in rebellion. When we, as Christians, ignore the law to love others, we have hardened our heart toward people and toward God.

Friends of God

In John 15:14 Jesus said, "Ye are My friends, if ye do whatsoever I command you." Jesus' family does His will. His friends keep His commandments.

That means we're not a friend of God unless we do what He commands us to do.

Jesus wants us to be a part of His family and then friends to each other. Some people are of the same family, but they're not friends. You may have this same problem in your natural family. There are certain members you are closer to than others. You have more in common with them, or you get along with them better, or you spend more time with them and have gotten to know them better. You aren't just family, you are friends as well.

God called Moses and Abraham His friends (Exodus 33:11; James 2:23). Jesus referred to Lazarus as His friend (John 11:11). As a result of their friendship with the Lord, these men enjoyed a special closeness and communion with Him. Jesus extends that same privilege to every one of us who will keep His commandments. He said, "Henceforth I call you not servants...but I have called you friends" (John 15:15).

Many of us in the Body of Christ aren't doing the Word of God. We're saved, but we don't have a strong relationship and God can't trust us. God can only trust us if we do what He says to do.

Imagine giving your twenty-year-old son $5,000 and saying, "I'm giving this money to you to invest. If you can take care of this amount responsibly, then we'll work on another deal." He invests it wisely and makes money and you're able to trust him and give him more money. In much the same way, we grow in God as we listen to Him and obey Him and show Him we can be trusted.

The Word of God gives us instructions about what we should and should not do. The more we hear it and take it into our lives and do it, the more we can be trusted. God's Word is true, regardless of whether we do it or not. It's the unchanging Word and we will see it more as we do it more.

We want a strong relationship with Jesus. We want to walk in wisdom, strength, love, and peace. The more we hear and do, the more Jesus becomes clear to us.

Do the Word

If we would take Jesus at His Word, our lives would be so much brighter and better. If He says, "Don't worry," then we shouldn't worry. If He says, "Pray and believe," then we should pray and believe. If He says, "I give you power and authority," we have power and authority.

As we read Scriptures, we will get stronger in the Lord and will get more knowledge about what He expects from us. We will be able to see more clearly and know how to live a life pleasing to God. Our lives will be a reflection of Jesus. The more we put our faith in His authority, the more victory we will have in life.

Unfortunately, many Christians do not want to submit to authority. We want to be rebellious. We don't want to walk in love or obedience. Rebellious Christians are not going to enjoy a close, family relationship with the Lord.

Hardness of heart often produces rebellion. The Greek word translated as hardness of heart in the Bible means "destitute of spiritual perception." It keeps people from seeing in a spiritual way.

Hardness of heart caused my ancestors to wander in the wilderness for forty years trying to get to the promised land. Time and time again they rebelled against God. They murmured and complained about everything. They even wanted to turn around and go back to Egypt. Despite constant miracles, which provided for all their needs, they looked to other gods and worshiped them.

They had no real vision of God. One entire generation of people died in the wilderness because they couldn't see God as the one who was able to take them into the promised land.

The same problem exists today in the Body of Christ. God wants to reveal Jesus to everyone clearly. It's up to every individual to decide how much of Jesus he wants revealed. Jesus still comes to His own in churches across the world, but all too often His own people fail to receive Him.

We shake our head over those short-sighted, stiff-necked, wandering Jews, but sometimes we are guilty of the same attitudes and sins that kept them from seeing God. We have less excuse for our rebellion, because we have the whole Bible to show us who God is. The children of Israel only had the word of Moses and the stories passed down from their ancestors.

We have the whole New Testament to show us Jesus, yet we often reject Him and His laws. Why is the Bible found in every Christian home, but seldom read? Perhaps we don't look at the Word of God because we are afraid of what we might see.

There are other laws in the Bible the Body of Christ is not following. If we are putting away or ignoring a part of the Word, then we are putting away Jesus because the Word is Jesus. When we are in rebellion we don't hear and we don't see. Just as parents know when their children harden their hearts against them and they're stubborn and rebellious, don't you think God knows when we "big people" are acting in a stubborn or rebellious manner?

The Image of Christ

At the beginning of this book, I described the way in which Gutzon Borglum created the faces of four of our presidents on the face of Mount Rushmore in South Dakota. He started with an idea and the idea began to take form in the rock of the mountain. With big drills and dynamite and scores of workmen, he went to work. They were chiseling, drilling, and blowing away parts of the mountain to shape the face of each individual president. Every part of the rock that didn't fit the image was chiseled away, until each face was sculpted in the rock. Now thousands of people come to see his finished work.

Before Gutzon Borglum began his work nothing could be seen but rugged mountain rock. We might say he brought forth beauty by doing away with the unnecessary. Borglum took great delight in telling surprised visitors that the faces of the four presidents were always in the mountain. As he put it, "The heads were there all the time. All I did was chisel away the irrelevant."

We can be shaped and sculpted into something beautiful by the Lord. He wants to bring out the image of Christ in our lives. It is a difficult task for us sometimes to know what is important and what is irrelevant to the true beauty of our lives. God is able to see what must be done to bring out the undiscovered beauty inside us. When we yield ourselves into His hands, we allow Him to remove the irrelevant. God wants to take out of our lives and minds everything that doesn't look like Jesus. God wants Jesus to come forth and to be formed in us. He wants Jesus' love, joy, and peace to be inside us and to be seen on the outside of us. He wants Jesus' comfort, wisdom, and power to come forth in us.

Many people get saved, but they never go on to let God work to form Jesus in their lives. They won't give up their "rights" in life and surrender everything to Jesus. That's why they feel unfulfilled. They are not bearing fruit for Him. John chapter 15 tells us that those who abide in the vine (Jesus) are branches. As long as we (the branches) bear fruit we remain fastened to the vine. All who do not abide in the vine, God removes from the garden. If we bear fruit, God prunes us so we can produce even more fruit. That's how the Lord cleans us up and helps us look more like Jesus.

There is a park in Tulsa where dozens of varieties of roses are cultivated. After the growing season is over, the rosebushes are cut back low to the ground. It doesn't seem possible for them to bear roses again, but the next year, in the spring, the bushes begin to grow again and soon they are full of beautiful blooms. Rosebushes need the old growth trimmed away so new growth can take place. Without a good trimming the roses wouldn't be nearly as abundant and fragrant and full.

God is the gardener; Jesus is the vine; we are the branches. The Father wants to cut out of our lives everything that doesn't bear fruit, everything that doesn't look like Jesus. God wants to make our lives clean, free, and clear so the fruit we bear is abundant, fragrant, and full.

When God starts working in areas we don't want to change, or when He asks us to give up something we want to hold on to, we get squirmy. We begin to move around and we don't want to go to church, because we know God is dealing with us. We are conscious of what God is trying to do, but we don't want to submit to the pruning process.

Sometimes, it takes the Lord weeks or months to break through our barriers. Finally, after He has dealt with us for a while, we submit and say, "Yes" to God. Then, after God trims away the problem area, we exclaim, "Wow, that was easy. Why did I struggle against it for so long?"

Some areas, such as religious form and tradition, are entrenched in the life and flesh. God wants to take rigid "religion" out of our lives so reality can enter. Jesus is truth and He is reality and the Lord wants His truth and reality working in our lives.

Everyone needs the same things in life. Everyone needs the spiritual salvation and the guidance of the Holy Spirit. Everyone needs emotional well-being such as love, peace, and joy. Everyone needs physical health, strength, and rest. Everyone needs food, clothing, shelter, and income.

God wants to give us those things that are best for us, yet often we don't seem to want the best for ourselves. We may be willing to receive salvation, but we can't believe for healing. Or, we may be able to accept God's healing but we find it difficult to receive His financial blessings.

There are many reasons we cannot receive from God. We may say, "It's too good to be true. Why would God do this for me?" We don't have enough self-love to accept the good things God offers us. We can't accept the love of God; we don't believe God wants to do wonderful things for us. As we read and study the Bible, it will show us what God wants to do for each individual who is willing to receive.

The Bible tells us God gives freely of all that pertains to life and godliness (II Peter 1:3). God gave Jesus who is our very life. Having given us His Son, will He not also freely give us all things (Romans 8:32)?

To know the truth about God's love and provision for us we have to read God's Word, and we must accept it. Those who think God does not want to bless them are believing a lie. God will not force them to think otherwise, but He would have everyone receive the truth for "the truth shall make you free" (John 8:32).

In reading God's Word you will discover the truth—God wants to work in us, to show us His reality, to bring us His love, to give us His peace, to teach us His obedience, to empower us with His strength, to impart to us His wisdom, to open to us His revelation, to guide us with His understanding. God wants abundant joy for His people.

Why don't we want to receive His joy? I think it's because we would rather hold on to our problems. If we will give our problems to God, He will give us His answers. God wants to work that truth in us. It seems one of the hardest things for Christians to do is to give their problems and worries to God. While we don't trust God to deal with our particular situation, God still wants to teach us to trust Jesus and not worry about our problems.

Chapter 13

God's Work in Our Lives

The Work of God

When we give our lives to God, He begins to work in us. He begins to shape us into the image of Jesus. And if we will keep our confidence in God, He will finish the work begun in us. Jesus will be seen in our lives.

Philippians 1:6 says, "Being confident of this very thing, that He which has begun a good work in you will perform it until the day of Jesus Christ."

Philippians 2:13 tells us, "For it is God which worketh in you both to will and to do of His good pleasure."

God's pleasure is to have perfect love, wisdom, strength, peace, and all the other qualities of Jesus in our lives. He wants us to bear the fruit of the spirit—love, joy, peace, longsuffering, gentleness, goodness, faith, meekness, and self-control. He wants to work His will in us. He wants to form Jesus in us. This is a promise to every individual who will submit his or her life to the Lord.

It was the pleasure of the sculptor of Mount Rushmore to work on that mountain for nearly twenty years in all types of weather and under all types of conditions. He was dedicated to that mountain for years because he had an image in his mind he wanted to form from the mountain.

It is God's pleasure to work in us, forming the image of Jesus in our lives. If we will let Him work in us, life will be easier. Struggling against God's will can cause the circumstances of life to become more difficult. God wants Jesus in everyone because in Jesus all things are held together (Colossians 1:17).

In our solar system, if the earth moved any closer to the sun, we would burn up. If our planet moved farther away from the sun, we would freeze. The Lord is holding the earth together, so it doesn't go out of orbit or so that other planets don't hit it. He holds our lives together in the same way. He is always looking out for us to protect us and guide us in the way we should go.

Mothers and fathers want to work in their children to teach them good principles, to instill in them responsibility and the social graces and a polite tongue. They work with them to study, to be diligent, and to learn. Doesn't a good parent want to put good things into their children? God wants the same thing for His children.

When we see children with their parents, it's often easy to see the family resemblance. "Oh, you look like your mother. You remind me of your father." When God sees us in Jesus, then He sees Jesus in us. When we're bearing fruit, He sees us growing and maturing.

The Apostle Paul interceded for the Galatian Christians, who had fallen away from Jesus, for Christ to be formed in them again. They believed in Jesus for a while, but then they backslid. The image of Jesus wasn't coming out of them and they didn't want to see Jesus clearly. They went back to their old ways and they weren't growing in the grace of Jesus.

Paul admonished them saying, "O, foolish Galatians, who has bewitched you, that ye should not obey the truth, before whose eyes Jesus Christ hath been evidently set forth, crucified among you?" (Galatians 3:1). He was saying, "You began in the spirit and now you're back in the flesh again."

Too many of us never truly see Jesus in our own lives because we backslide or we are lukewarm. There is no progress in our walk with Jesus and we do not grow in Him. Like Paul, today's pastors need to intercede for those in their flock who go astray so they will return and allow Jesus to work in them. Only then will Jesus be seen in their lives.

On the Mountain

Often our spiritual "mountaintop" experiences are followed by time in the valley. Here, if we are not alert, we may lose sight of God. We can be on top of the mountain one day, but, if we don't keep progressing, we can be off that mountain in a hurry.

Buster Douglas provides us with a good example of falling off the mountaintop. He was heavyweight champion of the world after defeating Mike Tyson. But, he's not heavyweight champion any more because he fell off that mountain after only a few months. He ate too much. He let his flesh go. He wasn't disciplined. His opponent in his next fight, Evander Holyfield, was disciplined and that's why he won the fight.

The Apostle Paul said, "Let him that thinketh he standeth take heed lest he fall" (I Corinthians 10:12). We can be on a spiritual mountain for a day or a week, but if we don't keep our eyes on Jesus, we're going to fall off and we're going to be in danger of falling away from the Lord. He will not be seen in our lives because we won't see Him as we should.

In First Kings 18 and 19, Elijah called fire down from heaven in a mighty display of God's power. Then Jezebel sent a message to Elijah saying, "I'm going to take your life" (I Kings 19:2). He took his eyes off God, who brought down the fire, and saw only the words in Jezebel's letter. He ran away in fear and God had to work to bring him back to the place he needed to be.

We get into trouble when we forget to keep building on the foundation of God's Word and applying the principles of success that brought us to the mountain. Jesus brought us to the mountaintop and, as we grow in the knowledge of Him through God's Word, God, through the Holy Spirit, keeps us from falling into the valley. With our light visible from the mountaintop, others can see that Jesus is growing in us and through us.

In the Old Testament, Joseph went before Pharaoh because the Egyptian king needed an interpreter for his dreams. After Joseph interpreted the dreams of Pharaoh, the Egyptian leader looked at him and saw that Joseph was different. He said to his counselors, "Can we find anyone in the kingdom who has the Spirit of God in him as this young man has?" Pharaoh, a heathen king, recognized the Spirit in Joseph, a Spirit that was different from the spirit in his magicians. Pharaoh knew God was in Joseph. (See Genesis 41.)

That's what God wants for us today. God wants to come forth in us so, when we meet people or talk with people, they will know we are different because God is in us. They will be able to see Jesus by the joy and peace shining in our lives.

Blossom in Love

When people say, "I've been watching you for a while and there's something different about you," what they are saying is, "I see God in you." People will see it, when we let Jesus blossom in us like a flower. Wouldn't it be terrible to have flower bushes that never blossomed? God wants us to blossom more and more and more in all the areas of our lives.

I've had many people say to me, "I truly want God's will." When I show them a Scripture and say, "This is what His will says you need to do," they start saying, "Oh, I don't want to do that."

"Do you want the will of God?" I ask.

"Yes, but that's too hard. I can't do it,"they reply.

They don't want God's will. They want God's permission. The Bible says the commandments of God are "not grievous" (I John 5:3). The only time we will have trouble with God's will is when we are in rebellion against it. Our human nature is contrary to God's nature. That is why we must "crucify" the flesh and walk in the Spirit.

Some people also say to me, "It's my nature to be this way." I tell these people, "We have a different nature when we become Christians. We have Jesus in us. Things are changing inside. God can change things that we think can't be changed in us."

The Apostle Paul is the perfect example. He was like a raging grizzly bear, who said, "Let me at those Christians. I want to throw them into prison." He had hate and murder in his heart. Then, when Paul submitted his life to the Lord, God changed him and Paul was ready to lay down his life for the Lord and his fellow Christians.

"Oh, you mean if I submit, things will be easier for me?" people ask.

"Things will be much easier," I reply.

One day God spoke to His prophet Jonah to go to Nineveh and preach repentance. Jonah rebelled and went the other way, and, before he knew it, he was in the stormy ocean in the belly of a whale.

God had a message for Nineveh and He wanted Jonah to obey and to go to Nineveh as His messenger. For his own reasons, Jonah didn't want to do it. Life in the belly of a whale woke him up and convinced him to follow God's instructions. God has a way of dealing with us if we don't want to wake up and do His will. It's always so much easier to obey God from the start. God will give us grace to overcome the tough areas. God will give us new desires for Him, when we don't think we can change. The devil does not want God to work in us. He whispers lies and excuses: "You can't change. You've been like this for thirty years." He tries to bombard our mind so we will not allow God to shape us and sculpt us into the image of Jesus.

The more Christ is formed in us, the more victory we have over the devil and the more power we will have to destroy his evil works. The devil's objective is to stop people from growing in Jesus. He doesn't want Christ to come forth out of people, which is God's desire. The spiritual man, at times, is closed, like the flower, and he has to bloom.

The devil brings fiery darts, sometimes through our own family members, to keep us from growing in Jesus. When I became a Christian, my mother thought I had gone crazy. The more I talked about Jesus, the more she threw things at me and pulled my hair and yelled and screamed. I had to remain determined to grow in Jesus.

The Bible tells us to rejoice and be exceedingly glad when we suffer such persecution for righteousness' sake (Matthew 5:10-12). He wants us to blossom and to bear fruit. If we get depressed when the family rejects us, it can discourage us from continuing on with God and growing in Him and His Word. We should rejoice when persecution comes.

We should also intercede for one another that Christ will be formed in each of us. When our fellow Christians are having problems, when they don't think they can go on, pray for them. God will release in them a new desire, a new love and a new determination to go on and grow with Jesus.

Ephesians 1:17 is a prayer Paul prayed for the Christians at Ephesus but it could be for us as well. "That the God of our Lord Jesus Christ, the Father of glory, may give unto you the spirit of wisdom, and revelation in the knowledge of Him: the eyes of your understanding being enlightened; that ye may know what is the hope of His calling, and what the riches of the glory of His inheritance in the saints."

Paul is praying that our spiritual eyes will be open, so we can see the hope of the Lord's calling and what God has for us in Jesus. We can see Jesus in many ways, but one of the best and most important ways to see Him is within ourselves. If Jesus can be seen in us, then we have caught a clear vision of Him.

How do we see Jesus in one another? We won't see Jesus in everyone. Jesus is seen in those who have surrendered their lives to Him so His glory can shine through them. Jesus is seen in those who follow His laws, do His will, keep His commandments. His image and likeness is formed in us when we give everything to Him.

Chapter 14

Jesus' Kingdom

Seeing the Kingdom

Now that the importance of seeing Jesus clearly is established and now that we recognize the need to see Jesus within ourselves, I want to turn to the broader picture of seeing ourselves within the kingdom of Jesus.

When Nicodemus, a leader of the Pharisees, came to Jesus one night Jesus showed him the way to see the kingdom of God saying, "Except a man be born again, he cannot see the kingdom of God" (John 3:3). Like Nicodemus, unless we are born again we cannot see the kingdom. Seeing the kingdom is the third and final aspect of seeing clearly.

Many of us may see God or Jesus in the pages of the Bible, but we have a difficult time seeing His kingdom. Perhaps even more difficult is seeing ourselves functioning within that kingdom.

When Nicodemus heard Jesus' words "born again," he could only think in physical terms. He asked the question, "How can a man be born when he is old? Can he enter the second time into his mother's womb, and be born?" (John 3:4). Jesus answered him and explained that He had been speaking in a spiritual sense. "That which is born of the flesh is flesh," He said, "and that which is born of the Spirit is spirit" (John 3:6). The kingdom of God is a spiritual kingdom. It cannot be seen with our physical eyes. It must be experienced within our heart.

Jesus went on to say that seeing the kingdom was not the result of physical observation. It could not be pointed to as being here or there. The residing place for the kingdom Jesus spoke of was within the heart of each individual (Luke 17:20). To see the kingdom is the function of spiritual eyesight, which is opened when we are born again.

A failure to understand the kingdom often confused the disciples. Jesus talked about the kingdom so frequently in His preaching and in the parables that the disciples expected Him to establish an earthly kingdom. When He died without fulfilling their expectations, their faith was destroyed.

Their hopes to sit beside Jesus in His kingdom were dashed. They didn't know that, through His death, Jesus would establish His kingdom. Instead of a kingdom that was limited by time and space, He was preparing a kingdom for all who would come to Him and receive salvation. They could be born into His invisible kingdom of the heart.

Since this kingdom is available to all, we can see the kingdom, just as we can see Jesus. We see this kingdom in the same way that we see Jesus with our spiritual eyes. I like to call it "spiritual insight."

When Jesus taught, He would often begin His teachings with the phrase, "The kingdom of heaven is like...." Then He would elaborate on some aspect of the kingdom.

Through these teachings we are given a number of specific views of the kingdom and those who are a part of the kingdom. For example, those who come will come as little children; the kingdom is for the righteous, the poor in spirit, and those persecuted for righteousness; and, some will press into it with determination.

On one occasion Jesus described the kingdom as a seed the size of a mustard seed, the smallest of seeds. Still, like the mustard seed, the kingdom will grow into a mighty tree or a field of seeds that will produce a mighty harvest (Matthew 13:31; Mark 4:26). On other occasions He described it as a treasure hidden within a field or as a net bringing fish up from the sea (Matthew 13:44-47). He also said it was easy for the humble sinners to enter the kingdom, but hard for the hypocrites and those who depended upon riches (Matthew 19:24; 21:31).

The way Jesus presented the kingdom was shrouded in mystery as if it were an invisible kingdom. But, Jesus also said, "It is given unto you to know the mysteries of the kingdom of heaven" (Matthew 13:11) and He assured us, "Fear not, little flock; for it is your Father's good pleasure to give you the kingdom" (Luke 12:32).

In Matthew's Gospel, Jesus spoke of the gospel as "the word of the kingdom" and He described the fate of the word when it is sown on different types of soil. Gospel means "good news" and that is what Jesus came to bring us—good news about the kingdom of God. After we are born again, we begin to catch a glimpse of the kingdom within the pages of God's Word.

For those who do not understand the Word, the seed of the Word can be snatched away as Jesus explained in this parable. Perhaps that is what happened to the disciples. At one point Jesus asked them, "Have you understood all these things?" They answered, "Yea, Lord" (Matthew 13:51). Yet, they lost the words He had spoken about the kingdom after Jesus died. They were fearful and uncertain about their future. They lost the vision of the kingdom they expected.

Many of us today don't have a clear vision of the kingdom. We don't understand what this gospel can do for us. It will not only save us; it will give us peace, strength, knowledge, whatever we need in life.

Romans 14:17 says, "The kingdom of God is not meat and drink; but righteousness, and peace, and joy in the Holy Ghost." Many people don't experience righteousness, peace, and joy every day, but these are all elements of life in the kingdom, a kingdom that can be within us. The opportunity to be a member of the kingdom is available now. We don't have to wait for the kingdom to come sometime in the future.

Once we begin to see the kingdom, we are to pursue kingdom principles. In Romans 14:18-19, the Apostle Paul went on to say "For he that in these things serveth Christ is acceptable of God, and approved of men. Let us therefore follow after the things which make for peace, and things wherewith one may edify another." These are the principles that we must put to work in our lives just as Jesus is working in our lives.

No, the kingdom of God is not meat and drink, it's not carnal, it's not physical. It's righteousness, right standing with God, a right relationship with Him, a right attitude and our position within Christ. The kingdom is peace of mind, spirit, and body; it is peace among the family of God; it is a kingdom of joy, a deep abiding joy that is our strength in the midst of struggles. The joy that abides in God's kingdom takes us into new dimensions of spirit and life. This kind of joy springs up from within and is not dependent upon outward circumstances. This kind of joy brings more excitement for life. As we grow in the kingdom, kingdom living fills us with health, power and wisdom.

Thy Kingdom Come

When the disciples asked the Lord for direction in how to pray, Jesus taught them the Lord's Prayer. The prayer concludes, "Thy kingdom come. Thy will be done in earth, as it is in heaven" (Matthew 6:10). This prayer is our daily prayer—that the kingdom will come and that, on earth as in heaven, we will see God's will done. We hear the Lord's Prayer and we think it is a lovely song or a nice ecumenical recitation, but we don't see the reality of the teaching of this model prayer.

God wants His kingdom on earth. To accomplish that He makes His kingdom a reality in each of us. We receive God's kingdom by following the Word of God. We have to believe it and live it. The kingdom of God must grow in us as we learn the principles of the kingdom. Then we can overcome the negative kingdoms of this world—doubt, fear, unbelief, depression, and so many other things that would come against us.

What does it mean "thy kingdom come?" The kingdom is not a physical place found on a map such as the earthly kingdoms of Great Britain, Spain, Jordan, or Saudi Arabia. It is not a political entity with a representative in the United Nations. How does the kingdom come to us?

The first step is what Jesus told Nicodemus. We must be born again. That is the first key to citizenship in this heavenly kingdom. The next key to the coming kingdom is found in the following words of the Lord's Prayer. "Thy will be done, in earth as it is in heaven." When the Lord's will is done, the kingdom will be present. When His will operates in our lives, the kingdom becomes a reality to us.

Consider life in heaven. Is there sickness or poverty, war or hatred, violence or suffering? No! Still, these elements exist on earth even though they are not God's will. That is because God's will is not being done on earth. Vast numbers of people have chosen to walk in rebellion to God's authority. Each night we see the results of that rebellion on the evening news. Life on earth for many people is hell because the principles of hell—violence, hatred, death—are practiced.

For the kingdom to come, God's will must be done. We must practice the principles of the kingdom—experience heaven's kingdom here on earth. If everyone on earth was doing God's will, what would the world be like? It would be something like heaven, wouldn't it?

We can't force everyone to do God's will, but we can begin making the kingdom real in our own lives following the Lord's commandments. We will see the kingdom when we have done what Jesus said we must do. This is why it is so important for us to see our role in the kingdom of God. We need to search the Word to find God's will for our lives. God has a special plan for each individual and we can find it through His Word and His Spirit. God isn't trying to play hide-and-seek with us. He desires for us to know His will and to do His will.

When the disciples were walking with Jesus, listening to Him talk about the kingdom, they all had dreams of what part they would play in that kingdom. They wondered who would be the greatest person in the kingdom; who would be prime minister; who would become secretary of state; who would be minister of finance or another important position. They dreamed of an earthly kingdom of peace, love, and freedom and, with Jesus as King, the possibilities were endless.

The disciples missed the point of the kingdom Jesus was offering. Jesus was talking about a kingdom where the greatest in the kingdom would be the servant of all. This was a kingdom where the residents would go, baptize and teach new believers to observe the Word of God in the power of the Holy Spirit. Jesus saw an active kingdom, one that would reach into all the world with the good news of the Gospel. "Go ye into all the world, and preach the gospel to every creature" (Mark 16:15). Luke records Jesus saying, "that repentance and remission of sins should be preached in His name among all nations, beginning at Jerusalem. And ye are witnesses of these things" (Luke 24:47-48). In John, the Lord told Peter specifically to "Feed My sheep" (John 21:16).

Remember, for three and one-half years they had built their hopes on Jesus and the kingdom He promised. After His death, they were without jobs, confused and probably filled with fear. But, Jesus didn't leave them in their fear, confusion, and grief. He came to them and showed them what they were to do with their lives. As He instructed them, He made clear His teachings and their role in His kingdom. Peter and the other disciples found a renewed vision of what they were supposed to do in life.

When Jesus says something, we have to learn to believe each thing He says. Jesus always wants to make His words clear to us. So often, our mind is in turmoil because of wrong thinking and bad emotions. These things try to push the Word away from us. They will keep us from seeing the kingdom just as they keep us from seeing Christ.

Today, we often do not see the kingdom functioning in our lives because of religious spirits, hardness of heart, pride, and fear that satan brings against us. I sometimes think many of us don't want to see the kingdom. We must realize the kingdom of God is not a passive thing. The kingdom of God is active—it is action, it is an attitude, and it is the condition of our heart. It requires something of us. If we truly see the kingdom, we will have to see what God expects us to do for Him. We will have to find our role in His kingdom.

God Guides by Peace

After His resurrection, Jesus walked into the Upper Room and stood in the midst of a group of frightened followers. For their fear he offered "Peace" (Luke 24:36). Suddenly, the disciples saw Jesus clearly, perhaps more clearly than they ever had before. He spoke peace to them because they had been troubled and fearful. He gave them directions for continuing the ministry He had begun.

God always guides us by peace, because Jesus is the Prince of Peace. If something is working in our emotions and in our body, shoving, pushing and creating fear and turmoil, it is not from God. We don't have to accept these things. If peace is not there, we have the authority of Jesus to rebuke the intruder and refuse to believe it.

After I became a Christian, God told me I would go around the world as an evangelist and as I went, healings and miracles would accompany my ministry. At the time, He told me many other things, but I didn't understand them all. Having been raised in Judaism, I didn't even know what an evangelist was, but I felt a peace about what God was showing me. I prayed, "God, I know You are talking to me. I don't understand everything You are saying, but lead me, guide me, teach me, show me and I'll do my best for You."

Many times in the years since then the devil tried to take that vision from me. He tried to take that light. But, the more he tried to take it, the stronger the vision grew, because I knew God had spoken to me. Even though I didn't understand everything and even though I didn't know I had the authority, I still believed what God told me.

We have to let God's words burn in our heart. When we truly know God is speaking to us, there is an unshakable peace that will take us through whatever opposition we may face. Philippians 4:9 says, "Those things, which ye have both learned, and received, and heard, and seen in me, do: and the God of peace shall be with you."

Follow Me

Each of us has a purpose in life. We each have a special role in God's kingdom. He has a plan for everyone who will follow Him. I can't give specific directions about what your life should be. Only God can do that. But, I can sum up in two words what everyone's role in the kingdom is to be. Those two words are, "Follow Jesus."

It was Jesus who first said those words. When He called the twelve disciples, He said, "Follow Me." To Peter and Andrew who were casting a net into the Sea of Galilee, Jesus said, "Follow me, and I will make you fishers of men" (Matthew 4:19). Immediately, they left their nets and followed Him.

Matthew left his job as a tax collector, Peter left his job as fisherman and each apostle abandoned their way of life and responded to Jesus' call. To follow Jesus is the same call we have received for we are His disciples also. In fact, the word disciple means, "one who follows." If we want to play a part in the kingdom, we must be willing to follow. What is following Jesus? It is obedience to His Word and the Holy Spirit.

To follow means to pursue, to come next, to come after, to succeed. Jesus asks us to get to know Him and to follow Him. Whether we follow Jesus or not we will be following someone or something in our lives—wisdom, influence, feelings, thoughts, impressions—sometimes it's good, sometimes it's bad. The best person to follow is Jesus. The best principles to follow are kingdom principles.

In the game of follow the leader, it is important to do exactly what the leader does. To do exactly what Jesus does we must have love, determination, daring, courage, fearlessness, sacrifice, and selflessness if we want to see Him and see where He is leading us. There may be times when we might not see as clearly as we would like, but we continue following out of trust and love. The effort is great, but the rewards are enormous.

Once we have made the choice to follow, there can be no turning back. Jesus reminded us to,"Remember Lot's wife." She did not heed the warning "Don't look back" and she became a pillar of salt. There is nothing to be gained by turning back from following Jesus. We must "follow on to know the Lord" (Hosea 6:3), keeping our eyes firmly fixed upon Him.

Matthew 6:33 says, "Seek ye first the kingdom of God and his righteousness; and all these things shall be added unto you." The "things" that will be added to us are what we need for this life. Jesus said if our priorities are straight and we are seeking to find our place in God's kingdom, then we need not be concerned with the material needs of life. Our Father will take care of us.

Seeing clearly all the time is a difficult task for us. There are so many obstacles standing in our way. But, there can be no greater way of life than to have your eyes upon Jesus, following Him in kingdom living. When we see Jesus, in all His grace and glory, we will know how great life can be. When we see Jesus in ourselves, we will have touched that greatness. And, when we see the kingdom and seek the kingdom, we will begin living the life God intended for us to have.

Review of the Ways to See Jesus

Use this list often to remind and inspire yourself as well as others.

1. We must ask God to give us a seeking heart to know Him.
2. The more we love Him, the more He reveals Himself.
3. We see Jesus by starting in the Gospels and seeing how He acted with people. He brought love, acceptance, forgiveness, healing, and wholeness. He's the same today (Hebrews 13:8).
4. Let's make this our prayer every day. "Father God, open my eyes. I want to see Jesus."
5. We see Jesus when we pray correctly. We see Him answer our prayers. We can know that He is with us through prayer.
6. We see Jesus as He works in our lives. It's more of Him and less of us.

7. We see Jesus in others who are true—by their Christlike actions, the look in their eyes, and the expression on their faces.
8. We see and understand His Kingdom principles for living. They are the best way for every person.
9. Continual praise and worship of Jesus brings His love, peace, goodness, protection, comfort, and all else that we need from Him.

A Prayer to Receive Jesus and to Have a Seeking Heart

If you have read this book and understand more about who Jesus is, and you want Him to come into your life, then pray this prayer to the Lord.

> *Father God, I come before You in the name of Jesus, Your Son. I see and know that He truly is Your Son. I want to receive the gift of salvation. I ask Jesus to come into my heart and life and forgive me of all my sins. Cleanse me from all unrighteousness. God, make me a new creature in Jesus. Give me a strong, seeking heart to know Jesus and You, Father, through praying and reading Your Word. Do a great work of grace in my heart and life. I receive Your salvation and forgiveness. Thank You, God, for also giving me new eyes to see Your Kingdom. In Jesus' name, amen.*

A Prayer for Jewish People

If you see now that Jesus is the Messiah and want Him in your life, then pray this prayer to the Lord.

Father God, the God of Abraham, Isaac, and Jacob, I come to You in the name of Yeshua. You are the God of light who takes the veils off His people. Please take the mental and spiritual blinders off me so I can see You, God, and Yeshua more clearly. I receive Yeshua as my Messiah. Come into my heart and forgive me of all my sins. I receive Your love and goodness. Give me a searching heart to know You and the Scriptures, for You are the Word of life. In Yeshua's name, Amen.

How to Schedule Ira Kellman for Meetings

Ira Kellman is available for ministry in various types of meetings. Ira is a teacher/evangelist who ministers in a simple, clear, and yet profound way. God uses him in the ministry of healings, miracles, and creative miracles. There are results in every meeting.

Ira ministers to singles groups, marriage seminars, business organizations (motivational), professional sports clubs (chapel services, counseling), in churches, seminars, and crusades.

You can contact him at:

Ira Kellman Ministries
P.O. Box 35187
Tulsa, OK 74153

Phone/FAX: 918-251-4717

Cassette Tapes

Stirring, anointed cassette tapes by Ira Kellman are also available. Write to the following address for a list.

Ira Kellman Ministries
P.O. Box 35187
Tulsa, OK 74153